One Man's Journey

A Pastor's Progress in Discipleship

Mike Story

IMD Press
Westminster, Colorado

One Man's Journey

A Pastor's Progress in Discipleship

ISBN-9: 0-9788201-9-3
ISBN-13: 978-0-9788201-9-0

Cover Design: Becky Hawley Design, Inc.
Printed in the United States of America

Published by IMD Press
7140 Hooker Street
Westminster, CO 80030
www.imdpress.com

Acknowledgements

How do you begin to express your appreciation for the people who have helped you, loved you and assisted you along the journey? Mine will be an inadequate attempt. I begin with, and most importantly, express my deepest love and appreciation for my bride of 35 years, Dee, without whom none of this would likely to have been possible. She will never completely know what she means to me because my words are inadequate. I am so grateful that she is a low-maintenance woman, friend, mother and companion. I am indebted to Community of Grace and the elder leadership who gave me the time to write. They have been most gracious. I will always be in debt to Max and Sandra Barnett for all they have done for me. No one has done more to mentor, counsel, and support me over the years than they have. I am indebted to my two best buddies, Rick Taylor and Jim Younger who are, well, just my friends. They have believed in me and supported me for all these years, and they are like brothers to me! There are so many others that have contributed to my life: Dr. Ron Hornecker, John Crawford, Randy Shuler, Willie Isaacson, Dave Dawson, Richard Coss, Tom Boyd, John Vann, Kent Humphreys, Rory Tucker, William Golson and many others I can't begin to mention. Thank you to all who have helped shape me. I also thank Tom Pratt and Rob Norris for helping shape this book into a readable form!

Contents

Preface

I have just taken my father (91 years old) back to his home in Oklahoma City. We just spent a week together at our lake home while I worked on this book. We sat warmly in the home by our wood stove as we endured four days of ice and sleet that shut down Northeastern Oklahoma. My dad has been a widower for almost two years, losing his bride, my mom, of almost 67 years. She was 87 when she died. Her last ten years were battling Alzheimer's disease. Alzheimer's is a horrible disease that robs a person of who they are and touches far too many of us. My dad rarely left my mom's side and would never allow even the hint of placing her in a nursing home. He had married for better and for worse, in sickness and in health, and meant what he had said. While he worked, he was gone more than he was home and traveled all over the world, leaving mom at home with the kids. Now, he would not leave her side until she died. When he retired at 76, he was still physically strong and mentally very sharp. At 91 Dad is just a shell of what he once was, but is still sharp mentally, but as he says, old age has snuck up on him. I don't know how many days he has with us, but I cherish whatever time we have and will someday miss his stories. My dad is just a reminder of the verse found in James 4:14b that states, "For you are a mist that appears for a little time and then vanishes." This is our life, a mist. I look in the mirror and see the mist of my own life. I am the baby of my family, and I am in my mid 50s. Someday, like my mom and others I have known, I will stand before God and give an account of my choices and decisions.

It is out of my journey that I wish to look at a variety of issues that, I believe, most who desire to be used by God, will face. Some may not draw my conclusions or agree with my assumptions, but most will have to face the questions. I have met some persons who felt called to preach since they were in the crib. This book may not relate to them. Those who come from a long line of pastors may not understand the need for this writing, but they probably need to face some of the same issues honestly, though they don't sense the need. This book is for all persons who are amazed at the leadership of Christ and under-whelmed by their own abilities. Again, my view is from that of one whose heart has been captivated by the call of discipleship. I am a product of all my life experiences and am like a river that has been influenced by a multitude of tributaries. Finally, I recognize that my experiences and process may not be yours, but if you seek to follow truth and live a life that matters for those things which are eternal, I hope the process of my journey resonates with your heart!

Beginnings

As far as I know there was nothing special about my birth, except for the fact that I was the only son and the last child born to Floyd and Helen Story. I was born in the spring of 1952 in Elk City, Oklahoma. Shortly afterward my parents, two sisters and I moved to Sterling, Colorado, so I have no memories of Elk City.

My dad worked in the oil fields, so wherever the rigs were sticking pipe in the ground for oil our family relocated. By the time I graduated from high school, I had attended twelve schools, including three different high schools in two states and two countries.

My mother was the spiritual head of the home, but there was no mistaking the fact that my dad was the head in all other areas. He was a very powerful man physically, the epitome of an oilman. We were on the poor end of the oil patch, though I did not realize that at the time. Mom made sure all of the children were in church on a regular basis. That meant attending each Sunday morning, evening and on Wednesday evenings, all revival meetings and other church related meetings. My earliest memories revolve around church activities, oil rigs, the Three Stooges and Popeye!

Dad was my hero, my personal John Wayne. He was a product of the Depression and hard times in southern Oklahoma. He was raised on hard work and more hard work. I doubt that my dad often heard the words "I love you." When he spoke of his father, who had taken his life after losing everything in the Depression, it was always in terms of severe discipline and hard work. His mother lived to be over 90 years old. My only memory of her was that she was a tough woman, who rarely spoke and seemed to have little use for small kids. Granny was literally a pioneer woman. I can remember being spellbound by the fact that she chewed tobacco and a substance called "snuff." In fact it seemed like everybody in my dad's family chewed something. I had an uncle named Leo who would tease me by telling me to hold still so he could spit over my head. I never stuck around long enough to see if he actually could! We visited dad's family every summer. My memories of those times include the chewing tobacco, warm milk fresh from the cow with cream on the top, outhouses and fishing on Lake Texhoma.

While dad's family was close, the relationships were very different from my own home and from the affectionate caring love I saw demonstrated in my mom's family. Dad's family was "tough and rough." Even his sisters were tough! In fact one of my aunts could whip most of the men I knew. They did seem to enjoy the times when dad, who was the youngest of eight, would come home. A lot of "yarn" would be spun and lots of "whoppers" told, but those were great times for a little boy to remember.

As the years passed I realized something very significant about my dad. He had never actually had a childhood, a time to just be a little boy. His early dreams of playing sports and attending college were taken away by older siblings, who determined that he should not go to college but work the farm and stay with their mom after their father's suicide. I doubt that my father or any of his siblings ever heard words of love and affirmation from their dad. This fact shaped my dad and toughened him, but also wounded him. Later, even the farm was given to another sibling, whom the older brothers preferred to farm it, and my father agreed with the decision. Dad continued to work other farms, even one he bought, worked as a brakeman on the railroad, cut timber with his father-in-law, but it was the oil field that provided an out for him vocationally. As the oil fields offered my dad a future and new beginning, my mother's family offered gentle warmth, which he had not experienced in his own family.

> My earliest memories revolve around church activities, oil rigs, the Three Stooges and Popeye!

Mom's family was very different from dad's—they were always laughing and hugging one another. There would be tears of joy when we arrived at my grandparent's home, and when we left, there were always tears of sorrow. Mom's family would wave goodbye until we were no longer in sight. Grandpa Still was a kind and gentle man who loved his daughters, son-in-laws and grandchildren. I loved spending time at grandpa's house because I knew he loved having us there. He even built a Davy Crocket fort in his backyard, complete with a gun tower and prison, for his grandchildren. He took us to the park to play and to TG&Y to buy toys (always against mom's wishes).

On Saturday night, when we were with Grandpa, my cousin Ricky and I would watch wrestling on TV. The wrestling itself was really very bad, but being with Grandpa made it very special. From chiggers to the DDT trucks spraying the neighborhoods, life was very exciting at Grandpa Stills' house. With him I learned to love oatmeal and sweet tea—the sweeter the better. He always called his three daughters "Sister" and called my dad "FOS" (initials for

> Dad's philosophy was that mom would raise the kids, and he would provide the means to pay the bills.

Floyd Owen Story). Everyone else was called "honey" or "sugar," which was always expressed in love. Even today, I am called "Brother" by her family. I wish I could have known him as an adult, for I know I could have learned much from this caring man. My grandmother was stern but as loving as grandpa. There was always an abundance of love in their home, and I eagerly looked forward to each trip to Norman, Oklahoma, to visit them. It was out of this loving family, where affection flowed freely toward all who entered, that my mom came. Mother was a mixture of her mom's sternness and her dad's gentleness. My oldest sister is very much like my mom's side, and my middle sister is much more like dad's family. These are my roots, my family. I might add that my grandmother's maiden name was Spurgeon, and according to genealogy I have a distant relative that was quite a preacher in England. There is my claim to fame!

Growing up, I did not realize that our home was different from other homes, in that Dad was gone most of the time to the oil rigs. I thought that was normal. Dad's philosophy was that mom would raise the kids, and he would provide the means to pay the bills. I always looked forward to the time when dad was coming home, even though I knew I would probably receive a spanking for something I had done while he was gone. His first day home would be a day of rest, the second day would be the day-of-judgment, the third day would be the day of fun, and then he would be gone again on the fourth day. Dad was like Santa Claus to me. When he was on his way home, the house was hopping with activity anticipating his arrival. When he actually was home, we always had a lot of company, music and dominos. Friends both from church and the oil patch would fill our home with fun activity and cigar smoke.

The New Beginning {2}

I would have to say that my life has had a few markers that have made me and shaped me. My life has been affected by the way I was raised. I lived in three states and two countries, and attended twelve schools before I graduated from high school. Moving and the sense of never growing roots had a profound affect on who I am. The constant moving had an effect on every member of my family, some good and some bad. As I grew older, I began to be sensitive to spiritual things and usually enjoyed going to church. By the time I reached fifteen, however, I began to question the church and Christianity.

Moving to Europe in 1967 (we moved back to the states in 1968) was a major chapter and had a huge negative effect on my life. I was a young high school kid from the Bible belt thrust into a world experience that challenged everything I had been taught to believe and trust. This experience stimulated me to question everything I had formerly believed in, from faith to politics. While we were living in Norway in 1967, I concluded that sin was much more fun than going to church, though I continued to attend. For the next four years I lived the life of a rebellious prodigal son. I had determined that Christianity wasn't really for me, especially what I saw in the churches we attended. I never denied Christ, but I didn't think He was very active in the world's affairs. I was much more concerned about girls, parties, rock 'n' roll music, and the war in Vietnam.

In the summer of 1970, after moving back to Oklahoma in 1969, I took one short look at spiritual things in the Christian context through a Navigator-type Bible Study. It was led by Bobby Bender, then youth pastor of Nichols Hills Baptist Church, Tulsa, Oklahoma. Rev. Charlie Graves was the pastor, and I will never forget how he seemed to love me and the few guys who were with me. But I wasn't ready to change—not yet. The course my life began to take was vastly different from the way I was raised. Life became one big experiment, and by the spring of 1971, my lifestyle was beginning to take its toll.

The summer of 1971 was unforgettable! I had just finished my freshman year of college. I was on social and academic probation. I looked like something a windstorm had blown in. I was a 6' 2", 135-pound, hairball. I was something to behold with long bushy hair, tie-dyed t-shirts, hip hugging blue jeans, and a whole bunch of rebellion. Because there was no market for unskilled, unmotivated hippie-type persons, I was unable to find a job that summer. I had to stay in school or spend my vacation in Vietnam. There was a tiny conflict going on there, and I figured that sooner or later I would be going there and not voluntarily. I finally found a meaningful job selling potholders, oven mitts and five year light bulbs over the telephone for handicapped workers. I made minimum wage and a tiny commission. I was on top of the world, with no direction, no purpose and no money!

In August, 1971, I decided to go to Colorado to work on the pickle docks where cucumbers are put in salt water to become pickles. I actually never made it to the docks but along the way I did run into God! I rode with a young man named John Maulden, who was a fanatic witness for the Lord. Through John's witness and zeal I encountered Jesus Christ on that trip and surrendered my life to Him! I was in Estes Park, Colorado, when I was confronted with my desperate need and cried out to Christ to forgive me and make me usable for His purposes. I didn't know much about theology, but I knew I wanted what John had, and that was Jesus. I was taught to speak in tongues. I got pretty good at it too! I really don't remember the words I prayed that night in English (not in tongues), but I knew that I could not change my life, and I believed Jesus could. I knew from that moment my life would never be the same, and I was not the same.

Later, I learned that to truly be right with the Lord Jesus one must pray certain words, the Bible must be read, and that one must make a total cognizant surrender of every detailed articulated area to Jesus Christ as Lord. There, of course, is an element of truth in each of these presuppositions, though it is naïve and even absurd to impose an interpretive method on the saving act of Jesus the Lord. I knew I was blind and needed to see, was lost and needed to be found, was hopeless and needed to find hope in the only One who could truly give hope, the Lord Jesus, and that has sufficed to this day. I am aware that some want specific words to be recited, but the key is a broken and contrite heart that desires to get right through faith with Jesus Christ. Salvation is more about transformation than a specific prayer or which words are repeated. I didn't know anything about election or free will; I just knew that Jesus had changed me from the inside out.

Back in 1971 my theology was at its best, bad, but my heart and motive were pure. What I lacked in content was made up with honesty and a thirst for truth. I knew more than anything I wanted to follow Jesus, even though I wasn't clear what that might mean. My theology was a morphed Baptist/ Pentecostal type which at the time seemed to work just fine. I wasn't concerned if I chose or God chose me, if I had a free will or not. I just knew I was radically different. I had been transformed! At the core of my being I had come to grips with Christ's claim on my life. I didn't understand any theological dynamics at work within me; I just knew I wanted to follow my new Lord. I had no idea or clue what it meant to follow Christ, but I knew I could no longer follow me.

> I had no idea or clue what it meant to follow Christ, but I knew I could no longer follow me.

Following the event of my new birth in Christ, I left Colorado to return to Oklahoma. I couldn't wait to tell my girlfriend (now my wife), my friends and parents. To say that my new direction was met with skepticism is an understatement. My parents thought I was on an emotional trip and would soon change back. My girlfriend thought it was just another lie. My old friends thought I had found a new drug that caused me to smile all the time. My old college roommates had heard I had gotten "religion" and wanted nothing to do with me. Losing my old roommates was great, because the old environment would not have been good for my spiritual growth. My little dilemma was solved by a Christian who needed a roommate.

One of the greatest experiences I had in those days was seeing my best friend, Randy Mitchell, come to faith in Christ. Randy had been one of the wildest human beings I had ever known, and now we were brothers in Christ. Our friendship was no longer based on sin, and shame, but rather on forgiveness and grace! Randy's spiritual awakening and other similar events led to the beginnings of the Jesus People Movement on our campus.

During the days of the Jesus People Movement, I don't know that I followed any particular creed other than my hodgepodge Baptist/Pentecostal system that I was trying to accommodate. I did know that I believed that God could do anything and was in the miracle business. (Incidentally, after working in some churches, I wondered, absurdly of course, if there really was a God or at best a God who could do anything.) Some fellow Jesus People and I started a non-denominational church on our campus. It was on campus that I began to learn about intolerance. Adults began to help us, but at a high price. Some were "ultra-Baptists," who believed only Baptists were going to heaven, just like the Church of Christ disciples and the Catholics, etc. I began to learn that a person's religious background made fellowship difficult and sometimes impossible.

> We were bound by lives being transformed by Jesus Christ and the ongoing belief that God was doing a great work!

The college kids that made up the Jesus People were from every conceivable religious background. We were Baptists, Methodists, Lutherans, Disciples of Christ, Presbyterians, Assemblies of God, Catholic—while some had no spiritual background. Those of us that did have a spiritual background probably all presumed that everyone believed the same, so the discovery of our differences was sometimes troubling. My ultra-Baptist friends showed me a book, The Trail of Blood, which basically describes the true church of Jesus as being Baptist. We began hearing Luther being quoted, then Calvin (I thought all tulips were flowers!). We were barraged with the doctrinal baggage and positions of almost everyone's past, but miraculously we saw God keep us together. We were bound by lives being transformed by Jesus Christ and the ongoing belief that God was doing a great work! There was a lot of love, caring, Bible study and discussion, prayer, fasting, evangelism, and naively pure motives. For the most part we were Charismatic without a clue. Most of us were even asked to leave the church we started by our adult ultra-Baptist friends. We started the church, and we were the ones who attended in mass, but they were the ones who had the money.

During this time I also saw the best in other adult servants of God. Jim Morrison was a Southern Baptist and Director of the Baptist Student Union in Weatherford, Oklahoma. He didn't know what to do with the long haired non-church type kids that began showing up, so he just loved us and prayed for us. He even let us use the BSU facility for our Thursday evening Jesus Meetings. The Jesus Meetings were substantially larger in number than the Vesper services of the BSU. He challenged us to be in the Word and prayer. I also met a Methodist evangelist named Larry Jones, who challenged us, served us and encouraged us. He was the only evangelist in Oklahoma that we could find that would come to our campus and participate in a student-led crusade. He showed us faith and obedience. An associate of Larry Jones was an ex-con that taught evangelism, Richard Coss. He was on staff at First Baptist Church of Del City, Oklahoma. He showed us courage and giving. Richard has been a friend through good and bad. He was a true model of servitude (a word I believe conveys the New Testament attitude of one who serves Christ above all, even as Paul calls himself a "bondservant of Jesus Christ"). He also would witness to anything that moved and breathed. He was an inspiration to me.

By the spring of 1972 I was engaged to my girlfriend, Dee, who now was convinced my change was legitimate. We were beginning to see growing pains within the Jesus People, and sectarianism was very evident. I was also questioning my own "Charismatic" experience. As a result of my personal questions, I drew a few conclusions. First, my Charismatic experience was rooted in my need to have an outward sign to validate an inner reality. I no longer needed this validation. I believed in the Word and the legitimacy of His saving grace. Secondly, I concluded that any Spirit that bore witness to the Spirit was not the Holy Spirit of God. To clarify, the Holy Spirit does not promote the Holy Spirit. I based this on the Gospel of John's account, where he states in chapter 14, verse 26, that the Holy Spirit came to bear witness to Jesus and to bring to our remembrance all that Jesus said. I also concluded that the Holy Spirit needs no help to give gifts. I was coached in my experience. I find this is unnecessary and un-biblical though it is the common means of "baptizing one in the Spirit." The Holy Spirit is not a moped that needs to be jump-started. This being said, I learned that "Jesus Is the Answer." I learned that God can and will do what we cannot and is capable of doing far more than I can ever expect. I am a composite and a result of the holy craziness of the Jesus People Movement and will consider myself a Jesus Freak all of my life.

If August of 1971 marked a new beginning in Christ, August of 1972 marked another life changing experience. Dee and I married, and as a result we transferred to another university in the Oklahoma City area where I was able to find work. By 1973 Dee and I had joined a Southern Baptist Church. I would serve as youth pastor in a couple of churches until I graduated from college in spring, 1974. Dee and I moved to Colorado almost immediately when we had been asked to run a city wide youth ministry in southern Colorado. In 1975 we moved to Greeley, Colorado, where I again served as youth pastor. In February of 1976 another life changing experience took place with the birth of our first son, Jeremy. I don't know if two people could have been more excited than we were with the birth of our son. I was enjoying what God had done. God had given me the gift of salvation and service. He had blessed me with a wonderful wife and terrific baby boy. But more was yet to come!

A Philosophy for Living {3}

Before the birth of my son, I had been asked to attend a conference on evangelism at the Baptist conference center in Glorieta, New Mexico. I was on staff at Hillside Baptist Church in Greeley, Colorado and had been invited to attend a WOW (Win Our World) conference. So in March, 1976, a friend and I headed to New Mexico for a conference on evangelism. It was hard leaving my new son and wife, but I was excited to be asked to this conference. When we arrived at the conference center, we discovered there was no WOW conference, but there was a Reach Out conference, and I was registered. The Reach Out conference was focusing on discipleship and was led by denominational leader, Barry St. Clair, and a man I had heard about for years, Max Barnett.

I had always wanted to meet Max and had been impressed with the quality of students I had met who had been involved in his campus ministry at Oklahoma University. I was also very curious, because there seemed to be no shortage of jealousy among some of Max's peers and no shortage of criticism either. These attitudes had done nothing but pique my interest in meeting this guy who caused such reactions in people that I had no desire to imitate. I had no idea what was about to happen to my heart and what God was going to give me, but I have never gotten over it!

In a matter of four days, my world was revolutionized. I had been committed to evangelism but didn't understand why so many new converts fell away. I concluded they just weren't tough enough. I didn't understand my responsibility. I understood my responsibility as a dad for my new son, but had no concept of my responsibility for new spiritual children. This was about to change. Over time I had visualized that Max Barnett was a big strong athletic type of guy. Wow! He was a tall and lean mild-mannered West Texan, who was passionate about one thing—discipleship. He was nothing like I anticipated, but I had never seen a person so consumed for the fulfillment of the Great Commission as was Max. I heard and saw things that God used to transform the way I would do ministry for the rest of my life. Max taught me a philosophy for living, a rationale for what I would give my life to. I have over the years adapted and changed some of the wording, but the following statement has brought me clarity and stability for life: "To know, love and glorify Christ; to be used by Him to raise up qualified disciples in significant numbers; to help fulfill the Great Commission as soon as possible; and if married, to lead my family to do the same." This idea of giving my life to being and making disciples resonated with me. I recognized that I was called to do this one thing above all else. No matter what I got paid to do, I could always make disciples. I had never really thought that the imperative of the Great Commission is simply this, to make disciples. I had never heard the Great Commission before. I had heard it preached in terms of evangelism and baptisms, but never in the context of the proper command to make disciples. My world had been forever altered by this second most significant event of my spiritual journey.

> Being and making disciples had to be the center of all that I would do.

From this time on, what I did was not as important to me as why I did it and this statement clearly defined what I wanted to give my life to. I realized that I could do any type of work and still make disciples. Being and making disciples had to be the center of all that I would do. My life calling became crystal clear: make disciples.

Another significant marker event in my life came in 1980. I was sitting in a seminary class when I heard the still small voice of God call me into the pastorate. I was shocked! I really didn't like most of the pastors I had known or worked with and now, I thought, I am hearing God tell me to be one. I shared it with my wife; she cried for the next two weeks. This just wasn't in our plans. Campus ministry, youth ministry, evangelism or missions, but not the pastorate. I am not a mystic, but there is an undeniable mystical side to our great God. Though I couldn't explain why, I knew that I was to be a disciple maker in the context of the pastorate. It wasn't that we felt we were giving up anything; the Christian life was my gain; God got the bad end of the deal! I just had never thought of myself as being a pastor. Within a very short time my family would be moving to our first pastorate, but something was to take place that would challenge everything before we would make our move.

I graduated from seminary in 1980, which was another major milestone. The call to the pastorate, and even more the birth of our second son, Joshua, overshadowed my graduation. Joshua was born in March, a baby birth by appointment. Everything was on schedule, and everything was perfect until he was born. Joshua was born almost full-grown, weighing well over nine pounds. I noticed how purple and blue he was but had no clue that there was anything to be concerned about. Within the next twelve hours we discovered how critical our new son was. He was born with a congenital heart defect called "transposition of the great arteries." He had an emergency surgical procedure to allow oxidized blood to flow to his body. He would spend the next two weeks in ICU. Here I was, prepared to move to my first pastorate, confronted with something I was not prepared to face.

> Prior to Joshua's birth, I had really been in control, or least I thought I had things under control.

Over the next eight months God would teach me so many things about trust, faith and God's will. It challenged me more than anything I had ever encountered. Prior to Joshua's birth, I had really been in control, or least I thought I had things under control. Now this, and this was not supposed to happen to me! In December of 1980, Joshua had his heart reconstructed. When they took him to surgery, all I could hear in my heart was, even if I never saw my son again, I was to follow Jesus. That was all I heard. While Josh was in surgery, a baby who had the same surgery earlier that day died. Joshua's surgery was a major chapter and marker event in my life. Today, Joshua is a hearty 27 year-old man, no pun intended, married and father of a healthy little boy. Joshua's future is totally in the Lord's hands, and that is the best place it could be.

Another chapter or marker would be defined by the time period between 1988 and 1990. My family and I had moved to another state to begin a new pastorate of a church that I believed was a sleeping giant. Leaving the first pastorate was incredibly difficult—a decision I have reflected on many times over the years. I called it God's will and leadership, when perhaps it might have been nothing more than my own restlessness and need for bigger challenges. A little over two years later, the new church had doubled in size, we had baptized over 250 people, but it was like a war. I was not what the power base wanted. Every sermon was debated. I saw God do some incredible things but at an incredible cost. Many of the leaders didn't approve of me, the changes that were occurring, the people that were coming, and the direction we were headed. To them it was wrong, and I was the wrong pastor taking the church the wrong way. I learned a lot about myself and my ambitions and dreams. I learned about my motives and flaws. I also learned what a former pastor, Jack Taylor, had meant when he said the Christian army is the only army that shoots its own wounded. My evangelism professor in seminary, Dr. Delos Miles, had often said that rapid growth or too much change too quickly could have bitter endings. Dr. Miles was correct. After two years and three months, I resigned and started the church I have been pastor of for the last seventeen-plus years.

> As I expound on my experience and questions, I hope it might resonate with some and help others who may be asking similar questions.

It was the greatest failure and tragedy of my life. I was forever altered by these events. I had moved to this place to plant my life, and now I was flat on my face, a failure. I learned a lot about the body of Christ and how our behavior must break the very heart of God. I have often said that I probably never reflected on much of anything before the age of 36, but reflection has become a companion of mine since 1990. Though born out of tragedy, Community of Grace, the church born out of my resigning, has been such a blessing. In retrospect I see how blessed and fortunate I am and how God has been faithful despite my own failure. I have learned that His grace truly is sufficient.

These are some of the significant chapters of my life. Each chapter is full of stories and memories. The markers have shaped me and when I have allowed it, have helped me be the person God would have me be. Sometimes I have wandered off course, a little detour that ended in a pot-hole. Other times the correct road has been difficult and lonely but always with the assurance that I was exactly where God wanted me to be. I hope I am wiser now. I do see things with a clarity that once was nothing more than youthful confidence and pride. As I expound on my experience and questions, I hope it might resonate with some and help others who may be asking similar questions. To those who have known the will and mind of God since they were eight, I probably have very little to offer, but for the rest I hope you find the following chapters an encouragement.

Putting the First Things First

{4}

Go therefore and make disciples of all nations, baptizing them in the name of the Father, and of the Son and of the Holy Spirit, teaching them to observe all that I have commanded you and lo, I am with you to the close of the age.   Matthew 28:19-20

And the things you have heard me say in the presence of many witnesses entrust to reliable men who will be qualified to teach others.
2 Timothy 2:2 (NIV)

A disciple is not above his teacher, but everyone when he is fully taught will be like his teacher.   Luke 6:40

I had been in or around church all of my life and never heard a sermon on the subject of being and making disciples. I had never heard of spiritual multiplication, let alone that I was born to reproduce (the title of Dawson Trotman's little booklet). In the Jesus People movement, we had been deeply committed to evangelism and had seen hundreds of persons come to know Christ, but all of our discipleship was inadvertent, if not accidental. When I was a youth pastor, I spent time with some kids' more than others because they were hungrier for things of faith and more available. I confess I had no clue as what to do with them except share my life. It seemed so natural and right, but it didn't fit well with the programs I was expected to use as a member of the church staff. I had never had a pastor spend quality time with me, praying with me, studying Scripture or teaching me anything. I got fed like everyone else on Sundays, evangelism conferences, etc. But I had never heard of intentional life-on-life discipleship, except for the short time I had been around Bob Bender at Nichols Hills Baptist Church.

In 1976 I was introduced to my calling and purpose. Through Max Barnett and Barry St. Clair I realized that I was to be a disciple who made disciples. I was introduced to Robert Coleman's *Master Plan of Evangelism* and Walt Henrichsen's *Disciples Are Made Not Born*. I listened to tapes by Dawson Trotman, Leroy Eims, Gene Warr, Charlie Riggs, John Crawford, Billy Hanks, Jerry Bridges, and many more. My world became one grand journey of discovery. I had never heard these things. I had never seen the model of Christ and how He had selected twelve guys to be with him, and that those twelve guys changed the world. I had never paid much attention to Barnabas helping Paul, then John Mark, and how Paul invested in Timothy and others. It seemed so clear, and I was amazed that I had heard nothing about this from all of my time in the church and around the ordained. It was confusing to me that something that was so biblically clear and obvious was so silent in our pulpits. My amazement has turned to sorrow as I have learned that not only are our pulpits still silent, they are indifferent to the biblical mandate. We sooth our conscience by being committed to evangelism and even preaching the Word. We are even committed to baptizing folks, but we are terribly inept when it comes to doing the one thing that Christ mandated, make disciples.

> The outcome we are after is men and women who are disciples, who will make disciples, who will in turn make more disciples.

Even when we have gotten serious about discipleship, we simply develop programs and call a person a disciple whenever they finish the program. A program does not a disciple make. There have been some very good programs developed and written over the years. The Navigators developed the *2:7 Series*; a Navigator named Dave Dawson wrote some great material, *Equipping the Saints*; and Avery Willis wrote the best the Southern Baptists have ever brought to the table, *MasterLife*.

The problem was never the materials, but that no material ever written guarantees the outcome. The outcome we are after is men and women who are disciples, who will make disciples, who will in turn make more disciples. The greatest tool, the greatest material a person can use, is the quality of their life. Charlie Riggs, a man discipled by Lorne Sanny (past President of the Navigators) who served with Billy Graham, says, "Our lives are our ministry!" I would add that not only are ours lives our ministry; they are our message. Paul put it well when said the following:

What you have learned and received and heard and seen in me,
do; and the God of peace will be with you.   Philippians 4:9

What you have heard from me before many witnesses entrust to
faithful men who will be able to teach others also.   2 Timothy 2:2

Therefore I urge you to imitate me.   1 Corinthians 4:16 (NIV)

Be imitators of me, as I am of Christ.   1 Corinthians 11:1

On the last night that Jesus would ever spend with his disciples, He washed their feet (John 13:12-17). He said we would be blessed if we did the same thing. The point is that discipleship is one person serving another person to become like Jesus. It is one person showing, modeling, demonstrating, explaining, and practicing the disciplines of obedient faith for others to see and follow.

Discipleship is a commitment to biblical disciplines, such as Scripture memory, meditation, quiet times, witnessing, varieties of Bible studies, and many more. It is simply trying to live and reproduce lives that are pleasing and productive for Christ.

> Discipleship is deeply committed to people being conformed and transformed into the very likeness of Jesus Christ.

But all of these disciplines need to be presented in the context of being a servant. The key thing learned from Jesus and Paul is that all of the disciplines and concepts employed in discipleship are to be transferable and reproducible. The objective of discipleship is helping persons be like Jesus, to help them conform to the image of Jesus Christ. I think of another verse that portrays what I mean:

Now when they saw the boldness of Peter and John, and perceived
that they were uneducated, common men, they wondered; and
they recognized that they had been with Jesus.   Acts 4:13

The heart of this book is rooted in the main thing, and for me the main
thing is being and making disciples. It is my firm conviction that everything
else hinges on how well we do the main thing, and to date we haven't done
it well!

George Barna in his book, *Growing True Disciples*, says,
Unfortunately, the twenty-first century church has many followers of Christ in the sense that I follow the Yankees: We dabble in
Christianity. That's not what Jesus had in mind when He called
us to be His disciples. He is seeking people who are absolutely
serious about becoming new creations in Him—individuals who
are fanatics, zealots, mesmerized, passionate about the cause,
completely devoted to mimicking their model down to the last
nuance. Discipleship is not a program. It is not a ministry. It is a
life long commitment to lifestyle. (p.19)

Barna also states, "The Great Commission is not primarily about evangelism, it is about discipleship" (p.25).

Discipleship is about transformation. It is learning how to flesh out
Romans 12:1-2, "I appeal to you therefore, brethren, by the mercies of God,
to present your bodies as a living sacrifice, holy and acceptable to God,
which is your spiritual worship. Do not be conformed to this world, but be
transformed by the renewal of your mind, that you may prove what is the
will of God, what is good and acceptable and perfect."

It isn't interested in converts or numbers, it is deeply committed to
people being conformed and transformed into the very likeness of Jesus
Christ, that is what discipleship is all about.

What Does It Mean to be Called?

For those God foreknew he also predestined to be conformed to the likeness of his Son.   **Romans 8:29a (NIV)**

You did not choose me, but I chose you and appointed you that you should go and bear fruit and that your fruit should abide.   **John 15:16a**

In Baptist tradition the issue of one's call is extremely significant. The "primo" calling was and is that of pastor, while the "supreme" calling was to foreign missions. In this tradition one is called into very defined areas of service: the pastorate, youth ministry, education, worship music, missions and/or teaching in a Christian environment. This tradition is deeply affixed to the idea of "call," like that of the Old Testament prophets. But for me these clearly defined areas are problematic. I have met persons who said they were called into the pastorate before they were converted. I have met others who languished in a position to which they felt enslaved because of their call. I have met pastors who were adamant about their calling but had no communication or social skills, which were necessary for such a position. I have met men in the pastorate who were there because their wife was called to be a pastor's wife! Some tend to look at being called as being able to manipulate and control people in the church. So the question arises, what does it mean to be called? Does God call people he does not supernaturally gift to prepare them for his calling?

Because ordination is reserved for the "called," much attention has historically been given to this process of setting one apart for service to God. It seems no one dares to question what it means to be called. It has always been a point of interest to me that we spend so much time questioning one's position doctrinally (which is critical in this day of theological relativism), but so little time is spent analyzing to what God has called that person, let alone equipped him or her to do. Where do spiritual gifts fit into this issue of calling? How can we say one is called to be a pastor who has no communication skills or giftedness? How can one with no people skills be ordained into a ministry of serving God's people? If the ministry is supernatural, why do we de-emphasize the supernatural gifts of the body of Christ? Would God call a person into a position that he had not gifted him or her to carry out? Can we really depend on our seminaries to train the called if many of them really are not called to the positions for which they are being trained? I feel we make a grave error in presuming that we can train people to have the necessary people skills or communication skills that the church of the living Christ deserves. Man cannot duplicate what God alone can give, nor can we equip people for a ministry to which God never called them. The tragic reality is that our churches are filled with "right feet in left shoes."

I am indebted to the ministry of the Navigators, a ministry dedicated to discipleship, which God used to help me understand that all Christians are called, not just the elite clergy. It is my opinion that one calling is not superior to another, though the call may have varying effects and functions within the context of the church. It is giftedness that should determine what one's call is, rather than a warm mystical bag of untouchable issues. How can one question that another is truly called to preach, or anything else? I think the evidence demands that we pull our heads out of the sand and start helping people find exactly what it is that God has called them to. Is it possible to be called to be an honest business person, serving Christ in the market place? *Yes!* Is it possible that what one may interpret as God's call to the pastorate may actually be God's call to make disciples as an accountant? *Yes!*

If I may expound on something I believe to be undeniably true: *All are called!* To what are we called? To be witnesses and disciple makers. One step further is that we are all ordained to bear spiritual fruit, not just a special clergy or unique "God Squad." Among those who think themselves "called," we seem to have a real shortage of those who know and understand their calling to be witnesses and disciple makers. Can there be any higher calling than that of a faithful witness or one who diligently invests his or her life in others and by so doing develops lasting, productive fruit? Are women just as called as men? The answer is unequivocally, "Yes!" though some functions in the context of the church are gender specific such as the position of elder/pastor. If all Christians are indeed called, what is it that distinguishes and clarifies to what they have been called? It seems to me the answer is found at the point of spiritual giftedness.

One of our problems is that we pattern our ideas of calling almost totally after Isaiah and Jeremiah and less after Paul. How many ordinations and commissioning services have been based on Isaiah 6:1 and 8 where it states, "In the year that King Uzziah died I saw the Lord…and I heard the voice of the Lord saying, 'Whom shall I send and who will go for us?' Then I said 'Here am I! Send me!'" How many have been commissioned or ordained with the word of Jeremiah 1:4 and 5, "Now the word of the Lord came to me saying, 'Before I formed you in the womb I knew you, and before you were born I consecrated you; I appointed you a prophet to the nations.'" I am not saying there isn't a similar event taking place; I am just suggesting we tend to say these things about people that God has not! We tend to say a man is called to be a preacher because at a revival he was emotionally moved to follow Jesus into the ministry. It is irrelevant that he lacks the giftedness or abilities or if he even likes people. We just say he is called and ordain him; end of conversation. Then we smugly say, "Who do we think we are to question the will of God?" I am not suggesting we shouldn't consider the mystical call of God as found in Paul, Isaiah, Jeremiah and countless others. I am just suggesting that we need to help a brother understand what it is that God has called him to.

> Among those who think themselves "called," we seem to have a real shortage of those who know and understand their calling to be witnesses and disciple makers.

Spiritual Giftedness and Calling

We have different gifts, according to the grace given us.

Romans 12:6a (NIV)

It is one's spiritual gifts that should determine the area of ministry in which one serves. Frank Tilapaugh, formerly of Bear Valley Baptist Church in Denver, Colorado, was the first pastor I had ever heard echo these sentiments. Rick Warren, senior Pastor of Saddleback Community Church, has spent much energy emphasizing the importance of Ephesians 4:11-12: "and His gifts were that some would be apostles, some prophets, some evangelist, some pastors and teachers for the equipping of the saints for the work of ministry for the building up of the body of Christ." One of the great tragedies of our day is how we have devalued and ignored the importance of supernatural gifts from God to do his ministry in the world. One may come from a persuasion that the gifts of tongues, healing and miracles passed away with the apostles. That is fine, but what about the rest of the gifts? What do we do with knowledge, wisdom, discernment, prophets, teachers, etc.? In many places in my tradition a person could live his or her entire Christian life and never know or be helped to discover what their spiritual gifts are.

Many times we mistake natural abilities for spiritual gifts and talents for supernatural endowments from God. God may give gifts that work in harmony with our natural abilities, but they should never be confused. One may have a talent for a musical instrument or a beautiful singing voice and along with that God may give them the spiritual gift of discernment or wisdom. One may have the talent of being good in math and given to detail and God gives them the gift of service that allows them to be on the finance team at church. The difference is, one is a natural talent that any person, Christian or non-Christian, may possess, but the spiritual gifts can only come supernaturally from God, as he gives them to a Christian. Just because one is gifted verbally and a good communicator does not mean that God has called him to pastor, but perhaps his call is to be a salesman or politician. It is apparent that we have far too many verbal people who are mentally "vapor-locked" as pastors behind the pulpit. I have known pastors who had no time to spend with people because they spent the

> I have known pastors who had no time to spend with people because they spent the majority of their time in sermon preparation.

majority of their time in sermon preparation. What a tragedy that we are having sermons preached by men to help people with problems they know nothing about. This only produces sterile sermons by sterile pastors for faceless, sterile congregations. Perhaps God had actually called that person to be an accountant or researcher, but there was no one to help him sort out what God's call was for him.

The call of God should be evident to others—those who are sensitive to God and are able to confirm what they see God doing in that person's life. By being sensitive and lovingly honest we can help people understand what God is calling them to. There are probably those who are thinking right now, "Young man, we must not try to play the Holy Spirit." (I love when people call me young!) But we have played Holy Spirit for years by limiting the scope of God's calling and by forcing those seeking their call into predetermined boxes.

When I first enrolled in seminary, I was interviewed by the placement office for possible ministry opportunities. I was asked: "To which box (not actually) has God called you to serve?" I responded that God had called me to make disciples. The professor was kind and gentle with his unlearned student and explained that God only calls one to be a pastor, minister of education, minister of youth or minister of music. Those were my options, and I asked a very stupid question: "Where is that in Scripture?" It is fair to say that they had a hard time placing me in a "ministry box." Have we not been dishonest when we don't help the body of Christ understand exactly to what God is calling us to as individuals? How can people know what ministry of the kingdom God has called him or her to if no one helps them understand their gifts? It is difficult at best.

While in the Jesus People movement, I led a Thursday evening Bible Study, called the Jesus Meeting, at the Baptist Student Union on campus. At the conclusion of the study one evening, the pastor and the chairman of deacons from the First Baptist Church approached me and said that they saw God's hand on my life and felt I was being called to preach the gospel. They asked me to join the church, so I could be licensed to preach. At the time I was just hanging with the brothers in Christ in the "Jesus Movement" on campus. I joined the church in May, 1972, and was licensed through the mail that summer. Though I did not understand at the time what this meant, I am indebted to a pastor and deacon who were willing to tell me what they saw God doing in me. They had taken the time to observe me and, with consultation from the campus minister, they wanted to share with me what they saw God doing in my life. As time went by, I knew God wanted to use me, but I did not have any idea what that meant as it related to my Southern Baptist tradition. All I knew was that I was to evangelize and preserve the fruit. For the next six years I was fortunate to serve in many different capacities ranging from coffee house ministries, to campus ministries, to evangelistic crusades and finally the ministry of youth and education. All of these areas of ministry were used to show me what God had in store for me.

> If ordination meant something different than what I believed was taught in Scripture, what did it mean?

Though I had been licensed, I could not be ordained because I was not a pastor. This was tough because, though I understood what was being said, I knew that the Scripture said all Christians are ordained to bear much fruit and ordained to be conformed to the very image of Christ. If ordination meant something different than what I believed was taught in Scripture, what did it mean? I know it means to set one apart, or as a special designation, but somehow it has contributed to the idea of the "called" being the clergy and the lay person being the "uncalled." Is ordination the badge of being called or what? What God has called clean, let no man call unclean. Who God has ordained to bear fruit, let those who interfere beware! By the way, I was ordained in 1975 by the church I was serving as associate pastor. I later found out that my ordination was invalid in some circles because our Director of Missions was not in attendance and my mother actually prayed over me! (Some consider it heresy to have a woman pray over a man.)

I find it interesting that all of the questions asked me during the ordination ceremony were about surface doctrinal issues such as: "Where or when do you think the rapture will occur in the time line of the tribulation?" "What is your belief on the issue of speaking in tongues?" "What about those dangerous para-church groups?" I only remember a few questions about who I was, my heart convictions, and what I believe God had called me to. I have since been to a number of ordination services and I really don't know what took place other than we maintained the traditions of our past with dignity! Many men who have no clue about their own giftedness, their personality traits, or convictions of faith that will be necessary to make an eternal difference, are among the ranks of those I've seen ordained. I ask the question: "Ordained to and for what?" I've met lots of men who can stack their doctrinal position with the best of them but still seem to miss the person of Jesus Christ.

I am not opposed to the tradition of ordination, but I am suggesting that we should rethink what we mean by ordination. We should rethink what it means to be called, learn how to affirm the body's call, and celebrate with those who come to the understanding of what it is God has called them to, through a clear understanding of their gifts and themselves. If God calls a person to a particular type of ministry, shouldn't there be evidence to validate that call? If a person feels called to a certain ministry, shouldn't there be evidence of God's empowerment and giftedness? Aren't we amiss when we ask our seminaries to train people to have skills that God alone can give?

God Makes Leaders; Men Train Managers

You did not choose me, but I chose you and appointed you that you
should go and bear fruit.   John 15:16

And his gifts were that some should be apostles, some prophets, some
evangelists, some pastors and teachers, to equip the saints for the work
of ministry for building up the body of Christ.   Ephesians 4:11-12

"Is there a leader in the church?" One of the great travesties I see in ministry
is that we rarely know the difference between leadership and management.
In our culture one expectation is that pastors are to be leaders of local
congregations. How can one lead when he is not a leader? I have been in
many local congregations that are suffering from an acute lack of leadership.
They are floundering in multiple directions, creating strife and unnecessary
dissension, because there is no leader to guide. Managers manage and follow existing criteria and expectations for church direction, but that is not
leadership. When the norms are challenged, non-leaders struggle, as will
their church.

The most prevalent definitions of leadership describe managers rather
than leaders. Anytime someone reduces leadership to learned people with
communication skills, it is apparent that the author is a manager, who
considers himself to be a leader. Maybe he has a degree in management or
has attended seminars on leadership that have awakened the leader within.
Please! Leaders will make the hard decisions, the unpopular decisions,
the costly decisions. There is a cost to leadership that a seminar can never
address. There is a cost to leadership that a manager can't see or understand.

Managers will criticize leaders because they make decisions too quickly; they are too insensitive; they are rash and even have the appearance of carelessness. The fact that they have clarity, while others don't, or tend to be rather black and white, cause some to scoff at them, even discredit them. Whether a person likes President Bush or not, it is undeniable that he is a leader to all except those who aren't. Many of his political opponents are uncomfortable with his clarity of purpose, his relentless resolve, and his black and white nature. Leaders don't tend to have a lot of gray, as do managers. They make decisions quickly but not without thought; they just see things clearer than most.

How do spiritual gifts relate to leadership and calling? Because we tend to downplay the importance of gifts to one's calling, many are in positions that they were never called to fill, because our sovereign God never gave them the tools necessary to faithfully succeed. It isn't a matter of one's working hard enough or having enough desire or even loving Jesus enough. It is a matter of truly being called and equipped by God for a specific function within the body of Christ. Only God can do that!

> I have met many Godly managers who worked other's visions, but I've only met a few visionary leaders. The tragedy is that we often don't know the difference.

What I am proposing is not a position that is held by many, and because it is not held by many, we have a radical shortage of visionary leaders in the church. In my more than 30 years of ministry, I have never met a visionary manager. I have met many Godly managers who worked other's visions, but I've only met a few visionary leaders. The tragedy is that we often don't know the difference. In thinking of men I believe to be called and ordained leaders, I think of someone like Max Barnett who made disciple making a standard for campus ministries. I have also known many Godly managers in the pastorate, and I am not implying that managers are not equally important or called, for indeed they are.

We must understand that all are called to particular works within the ministry of Christ. Because all are called, all are ordained to serve in that area. The church must be specific and deliberate in its focus on helping members of the body know how they are gifted. This goes beyond giving little tests that simply reveal the obvious. There must be intentional mentoring and life-on-life investment. We must help persons develop an intimate love relationship with Christ in order that they may truly know Him, not just about Him. We must repent of natural ministries, which are void of any sense of supernatural power or any indication of God's presence. I realize that there is a controversy over the issue of ordination of women, and I stand on the biblically conservative side of the debate.

I believe that there are certain "called" functions that are by God designed for men , such as the role of pastoral leadership or elder, but the issue really goes beyond this. Whom has God called into ministry? All believers! To whom has God given gifts to carry out his ministry on earth? Every Christian! A woman in Christ is just as called into ministry as any man; it just needs to be understood in what context. I believe the Scriptures are clear. For example, in John 15:16, where Jesus, speaking to the disciples, says, "You did not choose me, but I chose you and appointed you that you should go and bear fruit." Yet, until we focus on what the call of God means and to whom it is given, we will usually just grapple about ordinations.

I remember my early church-related ministry experiences. I was "called" into youth ministry but soon realized that my calling was not as significant or spiritually important as that of the senior pastor with whom I served. The basic problem wasn't one of ego or understanding, but rather, reality. Ordination in most churches is a lot like the strata of difference found in the National Basketball Association, where one rule applies to superstars, another to middle level players, and then another one for lower level players. In the NBA you rarely see a superstar foul out. In the church the pastors are the superstars and youth pastors come off the end of the bench at the bottom level. I served with some men who should have been anything but pastors. These men didn't have the necessary gifts,

> I have actually served with pastors who just didn't like people, at all!

people skills, or abilities to qualify as a pastor. Yet they were "called" and ordained as pastors by a recognized church. In reality they were, for the most part, good men who had a heart for God, but who had never been helped in interpreting their call. I seriously doubt that they had been given the honest and critical assessment they should have received from someone who loved them. I have actually served with pastors who just didn't like people, at all! Their insecurities and personal limitations allowed for nothing more than an inability to manage, not lead and equip the church.

> What is tragic is that in many churches there are those who have a vision of what God wants or would do, but all too often, it is not the pastor.

They were many times crippled by their fear of failure, fear of someone knowing more about their personal life, fear of someone doing something better, or simply the fear of their own inability. Max Barnett has often said that fear is "God's warning light to trust Him more." Unfortunately, for the most part, they just live in their self-doubt and fear. Their fear rendered them unable to even trust God, because they could not honestly assess their own situation. Their fears revealed that, though they were sincere, good men, they were not leaders, probably not even managers, but for sure were not called to the thing they were trying to do so painfully.

The tragic reality is that, all too often, those who are called to other positions in the context of the church are viewed as nothing more than hirelings. They exist to please the pastor, to make him look good. In fact, they are many times nothing more than a pastor's "yes" man or woman. If you want to keep your job, do only what the pastor tells you to do. Never disagree, never think independently, never challenge your pastor and never have a vision independent of your pastor's, because he is the only one who can have a vision! The trouble is that this model has more in common with the world than with God and the Scripture. What is tragic is that in many churches there are those who have a vision of what God wants or would do, but all too often, it is not the pastor. I am not suggesting that all pastors operate this way, but I maintain that this is the rule rather than the exception. Staff members are viewed as very replaceable, while the pastor is "called." The staff are seen as mere hirelings, while the pastor is anointed and truly ordained. But, are not all called? Are not all answerable to God for their calling, not just a pastor? I don't want to suggest that it is only pastors who struggle with this, for there are staff members who struggle with the same insane view of calling and anointing, while all the while it is the fear of failure that drives them. I am not arguing that the pastor isn't to lead the church, and it is imperative for the buck to stop somewhere. I would never suggest that the pastor doesn't have a different context within which he must work out his calling. I am just suggesting that we have made too much of one and not enough of the other person's sense of calling.

I am indebted to a former pastor I served with, Dr. Ron Hornecker. I served with Ron as youth pastor while in seminary. Ron always expressed his appreciation for what I brought to the table. He regularly challenged me and made me better in my ministry. He let me spread my wings, but always with a sense of accountability. When I began to sense that God was calling me into the pastorate, Ron met with me on several occasions to help me work through the process. He asked hard questions designed to make me think through why I thought God was calling me into the pastorate. He made me evaluate my answers and the method I employed to determine my calling into the pastorate. He wanted me to dig deep and search why I believed God was calling me to this specific area of service. He didn't want me to take a short cut in determining God's call. After a number of meetings, Ron and the chairman of deacons confirmed that they had sensed God's call in my life to the ministry of the pastorate. I will always appreciate the process through which he made me work.

In all reality, Ron was the first pastor I truly respected (my issue). I knew he cared for and loved me. He wanted me to be what God wanted me to be, but I think he sensed I tended to take short cuts. Ron was a pastor in the truest sense of the word. Ron was not a charismatic leader or dynamic speaker, but he was a pastor who led the church with integrity and dignity. He was not intimidated by his young, visionary youth pastor. He didn't try to manipulate me into making him look good, but rather helped me become what God wanted me to be. He made me think. He challenged my rationale and conclusions. He challenged my thinking and my theological conclusions. He never let me settle for the cheap and easy answer. He was the first to affirm and confirm my call into the position of pastor. He has continued to be a source of encouragement all these years. I will always appreciate his role in my life.

One of the objectives of this book to help a person think about what it means or does not mean to be called. Max Barnett helped me understand all are called and that all have the ministry of making disciples, but that most don't respond to the simplicity of this calling. From Max I learned the meaning of Ephesians 4:11-12, "And his gifts were that some should be apostles, some prophets, some evangelists, some pastors and teachers, to equip the saints for the work of ministry for building up the body of Christ." Regardless of one's giftedness in their calling, their primary work was to equip the saints so that they could do the ministry and therefore build up the body of Christ. All I had ever known was that seminary prepared ministers for the ministry, pastors do ministry, and the lay person just does what is necessary to keep the church programs running. I realized that regardless of my position I was to equip the saints, that is, disciple them.

> The call of God is at its core, mystical and supernatural, but not beyond our ability to understand.

I deeply appreciate Reggie McNeal's work, *A Work of the Heart*. He offers some of the clearest and best ideas on calling and leadership I have read to date. McNeal's interpretation of the call of David ought to be read by anyone thinking they might be called into any church related vocation. McNeal gives a variety of models as they relate to one's calling. Some of the models are more dated but are still the preferred models of most seminaries. He presents a number of ideas of calling, which are familiar in circles of many young church planters. Bill Hybels and Rick Warren, whether one agrees with them on other issues or not, have also had a profound effect on how people are now interpreting God's calling and the role and function of pastor. They have at least brought a sense of freshness to the discussion of one's being called.

We must help those who believe they are called understand to what they have been called. It would be my prayer that our seminaries would truly help their students understand what it is they have been called to. To do this they must be willing to look past the box of their own theological conclusions and presuppositions. They need to help students understand to what it is they have been called, how they can minister within their giftedness with humility and the heart of a servant. Ask yourself whether you are sure you're hearing the call of God or the voice of a parent. The call of God is at its core, mystical and supernatural, but not beyond our ability to understand. God's call need not be a mystery with no evidence to help a person know God's will in this matter. Good intentions, or even denominational favor, will never take the place of a true calling of God. The key for all of us is learning to wear the right shoes. It takes an honest person to confess that he or she is serving in an area to which God has not called them. It takes a brave person to do something about it.

The Mystery of a Thing Called God's Will

For it is God who works in you to will and to act according to his
good purpose.   Philippians 2:13 (NIV)

I appeal to you therefore, brethren by the mercies of God, to present
your bodies as a living sacrifice, holy and acceptable to God, which
is your spiritual worship. Do not be conformed to this world, but be
transformed by the renewal of your mind, that you may prove what
is the will of God, what is good and acceptable and perfect.
                                                          Romans 12:1-2

For those who he foreknew he also predestined to be conformed to
the image of his Son.   Romans 8:29a

We are God's workmanship, created in Christ Jesus to do good works,
which God prepared in advance for us to do.
                                                    Ephesians 2:10 (NIV)

What does it mean to know and do the will of God? How can a person
experience God's will? From Friesen and Maxson (*Decision Making and
the Will of God*) to Henry Blackaby (*Experiencing God*), books have been
written concerning this issue. We hear terms such as permissive and perfect
will. From fatalism to rationalism to mysticism, all venues of Christianity
have something to say about finding God's will. I do not wish to get into
a sticky argument for or against any of these positions. I do have opinions
that I believe are within the context of what is written in Scripture. First, I
believe there are some things that are pure and simply God's will for all

Christians regardless of vocation, economics or persuasion. For example, I believe the ultimate will of God for all believers is that we become conformed to the very image of Christ. This idea can get lost in the circular argument of the theological fatalist as to what that means. It is God's will for all believers to become like Jesus. To me, this is a greater issue than where I live or what I do, because this will radically affect every other decision I make. Another example is that it is God's will for believers to be known for their love. What a radical concept! There are a multitude of biblical teachings which show us clearly what God's will is for the believer.

For example:

You shall love the Lord your God.   Matthew 22:37a

Love your enemies, do good to those who hate you.   Luke 6:27b

First be reconciled to your brother, and then come and offer
your gift.   Matthew 5:24b

Another example is found in 1 Thessalonians 5:15-18 where Paul says, "See that none of you repays evil for evil, but always seek to do good to one another and to all. Rejoice always, pray constantly."

The Scripture repeatedly tells us things that aren't just good ideas, but God's will! These principles form the basis for our understanding the purpose and plan of God in Christ for our lives. I am not suggesting that we look for things in the Scripture to fit our appetites or create some "mystical" promise that has nothing to do with the evidence of Scripture. I am saying that we must diligently seek to know what God's Word is saying and meaning so we can bring our lives into obedience to His Word.

I have often been saddened over people, who wanted to know God's will regarding a job or family issues, but had little if any regard for God's stated will in His Word. For me, seeking God's will regarding my personal stuff, when I totally disregard His expressed will on a daily basis, is an act of total foolishness. I am not saying that God cannot interrupt our selfishness at any time, for He most assuredly can, but it is probably more improbable than we think. Maybe a person is praying about a new car, but the problem is that they are buried in debt already. Having disregarded all teaching regarding one's tithing and giving, they still want to "know" God's will for the car they are going to buy anyhow. My counsel at this point is that, if I want to know and understand God's will for me I had better be diligent in honestly aligning my life to his expressed will as found in Scripture. In a nutshell, I am simply saying it is an oxymoron to assume God will reveal his will to a person when they refuse to obey his expressed purpose. Obedience is at the heart of God's will.

Again, I believe that the bulk of God's will is found in the Scripture. My obedience and alignment of my life to the Scripture helps bring clarity for every other aspect of my life. I am not suggesting that every text is always crystal clear. Obedience takes submission, prayer and the work of the Holy Spirit. If not, one simply slips into a form of Pharisaism. God's will is more than simply thinking clearly and rationally. It is also more than subjectively "sensing" where I believe God to be! There is a tension between objectivity and subjectivity. On the one hand the word is clear about the things that are God's will— period, and then there are the issues that relate to me personally. The latter part is where things can get interesting.

> One's view and understanding of God's will has an enormous influence on one's sense of calling.

Does God have a will for me regarding where and how I live? Does it matter who I marry or what I do? The answer to all of these questions is most definitely yes. But I am sure to disappoint at this point. Friesen basically says that God's will for our lives is in our ability to think and act wisely according to Scripture. Blackaby teaches a more mystical approach—learning to detect where God is at work with the purpose of joining Him. I think somewhere between the two is reality for most of us. I deeply respect and honor the testimony of those two men, but in reality they aren't like me, and I think that matters. It is very appropriate at this point to recognize the obvious: that one's view and understanding of God's will has an enormous influence on one's sense of calling. Because calling is so terribly subjective, it is almost always placed above the scrutiny of obedience, and I believe the consequences have been staggering. Back to the point, regardless how one sorts out the specifics of individual understanding of God's will for oneself, there must be a foundation of biblical obedience. Without obedience, what I do, where I do it and with whom it is done, is a mute point. For me, where there is no obedience to the Word of God, any acts that are presumed to be God's will are really irrelevant.

For those who, to the best of their heart's ability truly seek and desire God's purpose and will, obedience is not an issue. For them, it can be assumed that God will speak. Maybe he will speak as he did to Samuel, or perhaps as he did to Joseph. Perhaps it will be a burning bush for Moses or by the Spirit to Paul about what awaited him in Jerusalem. Sometimes God speaks through circumstance or other persons, but all of this must be established on a premise of obedience lest it slip into subjective false piety.

> Some spend their whole journey looking for signs and indicators to show them the will of God.

I challenge you to also be honest with yourself. What is truly your motive in a given thing, what is your tendency, and what is your history? I think it needs to be understood that for the obedient disciple seeking God's will in specific areas, there should also be confirmation from those who know you in Christ best. In matters of this personal interpretation of God's will, we need a community of friends who shoot straight with us. This is not to say that they determine God's will for us, but they assist us in gaining clarity and focus regarding the thing sought. Godly resources are those who love us, but (as Promise Keepers said) are not impressed with us!

The will of God need not be a like a maze in a cornfield or a needle in a hay stack. Yet, to hear some speak, that is exactly how they view God's will. Some spend their whole journey looking for signs and indicators to show them the will of God. Others look for only one, that narrow way. Both minimize the roll of their subjective choice in the matter of determining God's will.

My wife Dee and I have been married 35 years. We have grown together, shared together, laughed together, cried together, but always together. I believe I had God's will in the matter of marriage. I base this on the fact that Dee and I both loved Jesus and wanted his will. We were headed in the same direction and had the same spiritual values and beliefs. We sought counsel and prayed a lot! But in the end we made a decision to choose each other. I believe there could have been other guys that met the same criteria I did, that could have married Dee, but she chose me. I don't believe for a moment that she was the only woman and I was the only man in the whole world that God had purposed for each other. I love my bride and am grateful for the years we have had together, but neither she nor I

> Far too many brothers
> have made the will of God
> a matter of spiritual poker:
> God's will is clear if I have
> a royal flush or four aces.

were that one and only needle in the hay stack. I have a single friend, never married, who tells folks (with a grin on her face) that her husband was killed in Vietnam, and then with a laugh, says she never met him but is sure he must have died there (no offense intended to all our war veterans!).

I have an old and wise Navigator friend named John Crawford, who says simply, if you want to marry the right person, be the right person! I have met some brothers who have said that they are married to the only person God willed for them, and then they divorced. How is this possible, especially if I prescribe to a view of predeterminism? Far too many brothers, from Charismatics to Baptists, have made the will of God a matter of spiritual poker: God's will is clear if I have a royal flush or four aces.

The will of God is first and foremost found in the Word of God. Obedience allows me to be in a position for God to direct me in every aspect of living. God does speak to us about us, he has a plan for our lives, but it doesn't have to be shrouded in an almost superstitious system of discovery. Ultimately, God's will is about that which brings glory to him and what calls me to faith. God's will and purpose shall be achieved. The question is whether we will be part of the team or not. God's plan and our choices are linked at the core. God's will brings clarity and directive. I don't to have think I'm the only one, or special. I just recognize that God doesn't have to use me, but He has chosen to do so. God's will is particular but practical and though it will always call one to greater faith, it fits the one called. God's will doesn't have to be like a pair of shoes that don't fit, but all too often that is what it looks like.

One question remains: Do I want God's will and purpose for my life? If I say yes, for me, it begins with self-denial, cross bearing and following Christ. It means loving him more than any other, including my family! If I don't want this, I don't want his will. From my very subjective perch on life, it seems to me that so much of what I observe in church has been those who have said no to the cross but fabricated a Christian life that has more in common with Hollywood than the narrow way. Many, because they cannot blame themselves or believe that they are somehow not responsible for many of their outcomes, play a spiritual game of hide and seek. That must break God's heart. Personality plays a part in our understanding, but it must never be an excuse for a lack of obedience. God calls us to his will, which always starts with a cross—mine! So, do you want his will? Do you?

> And he said to all, "If any man would come after me let him deny himself and take up his cross and daily follow me. For whoever would save his life will lose it; and whoever loses his life for my sake, he will save it. For what does it profit a man if he gains the whole world and loses or forfeits himself." Luke 9:23-25

Church, Politics, Faith, and Power

Buy truth and do not sell it; buy wisdom, instruction and understanding.

Proverbs 23:23

The simple believes everything, but the prudent looks where he is going.

Proverbs 14:15

How many persons have come into the arena of Christian service with the sole desire of following and serving Christ alone? How many have discovered the sad reality that just as it is in the political arena so it is in the church environment? In denominational and church leadership there are many fine and Godly persons. Tragically, there are some people who lack true biblical integrity. Some have motives that have nothing to do with the Kingdom of God and everything to do with the domain of men.

Along the journey I have had the sorrow of meeting far too many men who are simply about their own agenda, their own reputation. They have been endowed with the gift of pride and arrogance. In my thirty-five years of Christian service I have met some Godly and not so godly men. I have observed as some very Godly and sincere men of faith have been over-looked for a position because they weren't part of the club, because they weren't from the right state, or did not have the right answer to an insider's question. I remember a young seminary student being denied a position because he used the name of his mentor, Max Barnett, as a reference. His relationship with his mentor made him undesirable for the position that he was more qualified for than the person ultimately selected. How many persons have been given denominational positions, not because of their walk with God or even their ability, but because they knew or were aligned with the right people? How many deacons have been selected, not because they met biblical standards, but because they had a certain job, or were worth a large sum of money, or simply were more popular? How many denominational positions have been filled, not because the person was the most qualified, but rather because they played the game according to the power structure's rules.

Denominations exist to promote programs for their churches, not cast vision. In my opinion, denominations rarely have visionary leaders. Vision does not trickle out of committees to the churches or from managers who have never dared to dream! Yet, because of power, denominational structures apply tacit pressure on the churches to keep in step, keep up financial support, and to play along. Actually, the churches should theoretically set the agenda for the denomination. The reality is that, over time, denominations begin to set their own agenda and the churches are expected, even if tacitly, to do what is promoted by the denomination. Far too many (one is too many!) denominational positions are filled by those who simply carry out the denominational agenda to further their own advancement. Now, because of the shear size of our denominations they must structure and promote to secure their own futures. Programs are developed to ensure the survival of the organization. The Kingdom of God is often spoken of, but the motive has little to do with advancing it. Rather the institutions of men become the ends that justify the programs.

> Programs are developed to ensure the survival of the organization. The Kingdom of God is often spoken of, but the motive has little to do with advancing it.

Denominations are not the problem per se. People with their own prideful agendas are the problem. How many persons have been wounded because of godless sectarianism? How many reputations have been scandalized because someone simply had the power to do it? Countless ministries have been blacklisted by abusers in positions of trust. Unfortunately, this is a grassroots problem, not just a denominational leadership problem.

There are some very ungodly men in positions of leadership within most denominations (most, because so many denominations have long since left their biblical moorings!).

Even in the local context, ministers who take positions in new churches must very quickly find out who the true power brokers are, if they wish to have any hope of longevity. Tragically, they must learn to balance what they believe to be the will of God with the agendas of powerful men. If they are unable to keep the balance, or their integrity will not allow them to do so, they will not last. Maybe it isn't a person, but rather unspoken expectations and traditions that are deeply instilled. It is critical for those in the ministry to find and understand these unwritten values, for they can determine one's tenure. Again, it isn't about the Kingdom of God, but the agendas and programs of men.

Some pastors take the next church only because it is the natural stepping stone, if they are to arrive at "the right church" on schedule. I have met far too many pastors whose motivation in ministry seems to be the accolades of their peers. They love being recognized. They love to be seen receiving their honors, but quickly exit, because they are too busy and important to hang around. They name drop and hobnob only with those that are perceived as being beneficial to their reputation. The tragedy is this characteristic is just as common among biblical conservatives as it is among theological moderates.

> I have met far too many pastors whose motivation in ministry seems to be the accolades of their peers.

Matthew 23:2-3 describes it well, "The scribes and the Pharisees sit on Moses seat, so practice and observe whatever they tell you, but not what they do; for they preach but do not practice."

I also think of Matthew 6:1, "Beware of practicing your piety before men in order to be seen by them; for then you have no reward from your Father who is in heaven."

Consider Matthew 6:5, "And when you pray, you must not be like the hypocrites; for they love to stand and pray in the synagogues and at the street corners, that they may be seen by men. Truly, I say to you, they have received their reward."

The thirst for the spotlight, the need to be in control or have power, is as old as humankind, but should not even be mentioned among us! What suffers the most when ambition and reputation become the main thing is one's character. All too often character has little to do with why a person is where he is. In fact, for many, character is a liability rather than an asset! When character is compromised truth is traded for what is most beneficial and expedient. Truth becomes relative and everything becomes gray.

Now before someone thinks I just have an axe to grind, I want to say that many, if not most of our churches are led by men who really want to honor God. Most of our denominational leaders are truly godly. But I have seen that, even among the most godly, there must be the constant resistance to remain pure in the face of power and control. It is amazing what money does to one's heart. Where there are power issues, there are almost always money issues. When my preservation is more important than doing what the church needs, I have succumbed to the problem at hand. When I promote programs that really only insure my position, I have exchanged God's purpose for man's agenda and the churches ultimately suffer. In the local church context, if I do something to hopefully receive the approval of my denomination and be recognized, I have received all the rewards I will get.

> It is amazing what money does to one's heart. Where there are power issues, there are almost always money issues.

In the local church deacons should be chosen because they are biblically qualified, not because they make a lot of money. Elders should be selected on the basis of biblical qualifications and holy integrity, not popularity. Denominational workers should be selected because of their Godly servitude and ability, not how well they understand the money process. Pastors and other ministers should be selected on the basis of their Godliness, giftedness and servitude, not because they will bring a higher status to a given congregation. Power, prestige, and control should have little to do with what we do. Power structures should be exposed and confronted, if they are not about the glory and honor of Christ. Committees should be filled with godly persons who can think, not just those who give to the stated cause or program.

Personally it is hard not to get cynical at times. I have watched those who can manipulate *Roberts Rules of Order* to accomplish their goals, while all the while violating biblical principle. I have seen Godly men chewed up and spit out when they were no longer deemed as necessary or beneficial. I have seen men in the middle of crisis abandoned because they were no longer a contributor to the power base or process.

There is a need for structure and order. There is a need for positions to be filled, but the structures must serve the people, not vice-versa. Positions would better be left unfilled than to continue to fill places with the ambitious and arrogant who seek only power. The only way a person can avoid some of these issues is to bury his head in the sand or live in a fairytale land. The most important thing we all can do is again die to self, seek his glory, and focus on washing feet, rather than focus on the size of our expense accounts. Prayer is central, and biblical obedience is absolutely essential. The sad reality is that these things are ever with us, and one must be skilled in resolving conflict if he or she is able to survive.

Conflict and Conflict Resolution

Barnabas wanted to take with them John called Mark. But Paul thought best not to take with them on who had withdrawn from them in Pamphylia, and had not gone with them to the work. And there arose a sharp contention, so that they separated from each.

Acts 15:37-39a

My brothers, some form Chloe's household have informed me that there are quarrels among you.   1 Corinthians 1:11 (NIV)

Finally, brethren, farewell, Mend your ways, heed my appeal, agree with one another, live in peace.   2 Corinthians 13:11a

Conflict is a reality. Change is conflict; growth is conflict; marriage is conflict; church is conflict; work is conflict; even friendships are conflict. Conflict is an ever-present reality that we are all too often ill-prepared to face, let alone deal with in a constructive way. Wherever there are differences of opinion, values or beliefs there is conflict. Conflict doesn't have to be negative, or worse destructive, but often the results are. In a tradition like mine, where churches are a type of hodgepodge congregational rule, there is always a conflict somewhere. Someone is always at odds with someone else. Whoever won the last vote at the monthly business meeting is subtly, or perhaps not so subtly, in conflict with those who lost. For some naïve reason I had chosen to believe that there was no problem so big that it could not be resolved through prayer. Wow! It seems so spiritual, so Godly, so biblically right, but what an incredibly naïve point of view. There are some out there that would still say that this is true, and technically speaking it is, but practically, it is rarely seen. Domineering leaders or tight fisted managers who stifle descent, are the first to say "prayer" is the key and that they work in an environment of unity and peace. Yeah, right! Their heavy-handed tactics are not a substitute for true unity and real peace. The fellow that follows these types of ministers usually has an unpleasant experience awaiting him. In an environment of deep-seated beliefs, strong values and supposed intimate relationships, conflict is inevitable. But if we are Christians, how is this possible?

The tragedy of conflict is that it is often handled so poorly, if at all. I suspect that many ministers simply leave their place of service or circulate their resumes whenever they encounter conflict they can't resolve or avoid. How many churches are vacated because of unresolved conflict? Some ministers have lived their whole adult lives avoiding conflict. Perhaps it was the way they were raised, or something in their past has made conflict utterly impossible to deal with. It is also tragic to realize that many conflicts within the church are over style rather than issues of substance. Regardless, if one is in ministry or simply has a pulse, conflict is an ever-present reality.

> Winning is not the desired end for resolving conflict, resolution and restoration is!

Conflict can lead to growth. Conflict can be healthy rather than harmful. Resolved conflict can aid in the maturity and health of relationships. Married couples who learn to work through and resolve conflict in constructive ways, become stronger and healthier than those who avoid, neglect or handle it poorly. Churches that embrace conflict as a tool that God might use to bring true growth and unity are always healthier. Those who want true unity in the church must be students of reconciliation and conflict resolution, otherwise they are living in an illusion. Winning is not the desired end for resolving conflict, resolution and restoration is! Resolution is about compromise; it is about collaborating, working towards win/win scenarios. Healing is a by-product of dealing with conflict in a Godly, holistic way.

Conflict resolution demands that we strive to understand the issue(s) of difference. In most conflicts the issues are rarely the same for all the engaged parties. Listening is critical if a conflict is to be resolved. All parties must agree on the issue(s) before there can be a hope of reconciliation. Understanding of positions is necessary to help each party understand the emotions and values that may be affixed to a particular position. One of the most common errors in conflict resolution is to assume that the issue is clear and all parties are contending with the same data. Often, nothing could be further from the truth.

There is also the notion that the absence of conflict always means health and the presence of conflict is always negative. The opposite is usually true. Peace at any price usually brings only an appearance of peace, when in fact it leads down a path of greater and more difficult conflict that someone else will probably have to clean up and deal with. Genuine peace is not the evidence of the absence of conflict, but rather the testimony of resolved conflict. True peace is possible only in the context of reconciliation.

I have served in churches that presumed they were unified and at peace, when in reality they were full of apathy and frustration. In one church the same five or six men made almost all the decisions, because they chaired all the important committees. Whenever propositions were presented for approval by voting, very few people would bother to come to business meetings, but the ones that did come always voted unanimously. The great majority did not care or thought it was not worth the effort to oppose the power brokers. When change began to occur and these men no longer won every vote, their interpretation was that there was sin in the church. "We are no longer unified; we no longer have peace," they said. The reality is that growth and change were bringing conflict that, if allowed, would have led to greater health and true unity. But because they could no longer control

> Genuine peace is not the evidence of the absence of conflict, but rather the testimony of resolved conflict.

the outcome, they opposed almost everything and blamed it on the pastor. Resolution could not occur, because they refused to look honestly at all the issues and instead entrenched themselves in the idea that the only problem was the pastor. Communication took place only in the context of lecture and debate to correct the pastor. It was inconceivable to them that there were other factors at work and that many of these factors were positive. The thing they really were fighting against was change and the loss of ultimate control. In the end it became a tragic lose/lose situation where everyone lost.

In conflict it is absolutely imperative to get to the heart of the issues, but it is equally important to find out with whom or what one is really having conflict. By this I mean that the obvious may not be the reality. On a staff I once served, a minister continued to bring issues to the table that rarely got addressed to his satisfaction and almost seemed irreconcilable. One day, in a staff meeting, he confessed that the issues were really not his but his wife's. The issues could not be resolved, because we were dealing with the wrong person. In many conflicts, especially within the church, the person presenting the issue is not the person with the problem. Until this is addressed and resolved, there can be no resolution.

> In many conflicts, especially within the church, the person presenting the issue is not the person with the problem.

It is also important to understand that each church's polity and structure plays into the nature and types of conflict that will occur. In a congregationally ruled church with regularly scheduled business meetings, there will always be fertile ground for conflict. Why? Because there are always winners and losers, and depending on the issues being voted on, conflict is almost inevitable. The more one has attached value or emotion to the issues, the greater the likelihood for conflict. In churches run by elders or even dictatorial type pastors, the conflict can be the result of frustration for being left out of the loop. Some grow weary of not being informed, and their personal history feeds either their trust or distrust. A wise ministry staff will work very hard to keep people informed and to strive for clarity.

Clarity is critical for conflict resolution. In many cases the disenfranchised just leave, but they take their unresolved issues to another church, and many times they become antagonists of change and growth there.

It should be noted that in some cases, if not most, there is a need for a mediator—a person who is trusted by all parties and who can participate for the sole purpose of making sure there is clarity and that everyone is hearing the same thing. The mediator has no influence in the outcome but serves an important role in helping all sides hear each other. This person may help by documenting specific statements and issues from all parties, to keep the conversation on track and accurate. They interrupt the process only to hold parties accountable and to aid in clarity. Again, the mediator has no role in the ultimate outcome other than one of assistance.

Another role that, at times, becomes necessary to utilize in a conflict is that of the arbitrator. This person, like the mediator, is well respected but almost always needs to be from the outside. As in the case of the mediator, this person must be neutral and without prejudice. The arbitrator is given permission by all parties to determine the outcome. The arbitrator allows a similar process to that of the mediator, with the major difference that his judgment on the issue(s) is the final word. He determines the outcome after all parties have spoken and listened to each other. Again, this arrangement is made and agreed upon prior to the arbitrator's involvement. The arbitrator's ruling is the outcome and the means selected for conflict resolution. Should any of the parties determine they aren't satisfied with the arbitrator's conclusion, they are in breach of the agreement and are demonstrating that they are unwilling for resolution. It needs to be understood that both the mediator and arbitrator must be wise, godly persons who are without bias. They must desire a godly outcome and seek with all their wisdom a resolution that is God-honoring. This is the desire but not always the outcome. When entrenched parties refuse help (and that is what these two tools represent), they are all too often prideful to the point of arrogance

> Conflict resolution requires honesty, a desire for a win/win scenario, and a willingness to forgive.

and therefore resolution cannot occur. Conflict is always an opportunity for healing, reconciliation, grace and growth, but the choice is in the hands of the positioned parities.

The fact that conflict is an opportunity for growth and maturity is beyond question. The fact that true peace and unity come through the process of conflict, is also unquestionable. However, one must never presume that all conflict can be resolved. True resolution means all parties must be honest about their position and motive (why they feel and think as they do) and willing to collaborate for the greater good. For those who must win or maintain control, there will never be resolution. For those who just don't want to work at resolution or choose to avoid the conflict, resolution will not happen. Conflict resolution requires honesty, a desire for a win/win scenario, and a willingness to forgive.

Of course, I am not talking about conflict that comes as a direct result of sin. Sin must be confronted in love with the hope of reconciliation and restoration on the merit of biblical principle. But it needs to be understood that unwillingness to resolve conflict always becomes sin. It becomes a sin rooted in the tree of unforgiveness and pride. When these take root, there are rarely resolutions to conflict, and the body of Christ suffers. When sides become entrenched or blind to their own self-righteousness, conflict resolution cannot occur. Reconciliation leads to deeper levels of trust and forgiveness. When conflict is left unresolved the opposite is just as true.

> Isn't it sad that the one thing Jesus said we would be known for, *love*, is often the last thing the church causes people to think about!

There is a crisis of conflict in our homes and churches. Love means that you must say you are sorry, over and over, and then change to prove it! Love is the motivation behind resolution. Love is the prime mover that leads to win/win situations. Pride has the other effect, the unresolved effect. The more prepared we are to deal with conflict in a manner that can hopefully lead to Godly resolution, the more effective our ministries will be. How many unnecessary and unwarranted pulpit changes could have been avoided, if we had only been prepared to handle conflict in constructive ways? How would the health of the church be today, if more ministers had worked more diligently for resolution, rather than surrendering, avoiding or being cast out to die? The data on unchecked unresolved conflict is vague, but the evidence is very apparent in our homes and in our churches.

Conflict resolution, true resolution leads to a deeper trust in the family, deeper understanding and awareness, and a deeper commitment called love. Isn't it sad that the one thing Jesus said we would be known for, *love*, is often the last thing the church causes people to think about!

In conclusion, conflict is a reality. Choose to be minister of reconciliation. Value the relationship(s) above all else (unless there is violation of biblical principle) and even then don't stop loving the person. Learn to be a good listener, who strives to get the facts and knows what the issues are. Work hard at helping bring clarity and understanding to all participants regarding issues, feelings and positions. Hope for a win/win situation with prayer and biblical obedience. Failure to reach reconciliation is not necessarily failure of ministry. When Paul and Barnabas separated, who was right? I submit they both were right and both wrong! They are examples of being rigid in their positions, but they were both true to who they were, and in the end they both proved to be right. The lesson is that sometimes resolution may take years, but if love is our aim, restoration can occur in many cases. Humility and commitment are required, and the process may get messy before it gets better, but the end product is a whole lot more satisfying and eternally rewarding.

The Importance of Purity

Above all else, guard your heart for it is the wellspring of life.

Proverbs 4:23 (NIV)

Stand firm then, with the belt of truth buckled around your waist, with the breastplate or righteousness in place.   Ephesians 6:14 (NIV)

Abstain from every form of evil. May the God of peace sanctify you wholly; and may your body, soul and spirit be kept sound and blameless at the coming of our Lord Jesus Christ.   1 Thessalonians 5:23

You have heard that it was said, "You shall not commit adultery. But I say to you that every one who looks at a woman lustfully has already committed adultery with her in his heart.   Matthew 5:27-28

If anyone purifies himself from what is ignoble, then he will be a vessel fit for noble use, consecrated and useful to the master...So shun youthful passions and aim at righteousness, faith, love and peace, along with those who call upon the Lord from a pure heart.

2 Timothy 2:21-22

It seems that almost every month we watch or read about minister after minister who has fallen morally. This moral collapse does not occur accidentally or just by chance. They are not victims. They are the self-fulfilled prophesies of men who have not guarded their hearts. In my present location I have watched friend after friend blow it morally. The pattern was always the same. The assumption that it would not, could not happen to them. The neglect of daily scriptural intake and the neglect of daily prayer are always indicators. The feeling that they aren't doing so bad or that their sin is hurting no one but them is very common. I have even observed some who felt it must not be as bad as some thought, because their ministries still seemed to thrive. There is always the breaking of fellowship with those who know them best and will ask hard questions. There is always a cavalier attitude towards moral boundaries and usually a scoffing at those who maintain them. The list could go on, but you get the point.

The question is, who is vulnerable? We all are vulnerable! Every one who serves in the name of the Lord is vulnerable. Our enemy, the devil, knows that if he can aid in the fall of minister, he can disgrace the individual and hurt the cause of Christ. He also knows us; he knows that there isn't a man out there who isn't vulnerable to moral failure. Though I know evolution is a godless myth, I have concluded that if men had evolved they would have come from dogs! No honest man disagrees! Let me put it in perspective. Every man can be tempted. Satan knows how to tempt you and me, and we aren't so special as to need special acts of tempting. Moral failure, either in form of adultery or pornography, is a testimony to our weakness and the commonality of us all. But here is the bottom line problem. Satan can only tempt, we have to be willing to respond, Satan only presents us with something we want! Consider James 1:14-15, "but each person is tempted when he is lured and enticed by his own desire. Then desire when it has conceived gives birth to sin; and sin when it is full-grown brings forth death." Only a fool believes he is above this reality.

> Satan can only tempt, we have to be willing to respond, Satan only presents us with something we want!

Paul put it this way, "Therefore let anyone, who thinks that he stands take heed lest he fall" (1 Corinthians 10:12). Paul goes on to say that God always provides a way to escape temptation. Why would he say these things? Because we are vulnerable! Escape is a choice; it is always a choice! God wants it, but do we? If we are taking short cuts or believe we are exceptions to the rule we have chosen to fall, plain and simple. This doesn't mean it will happen overnight. How many nights did King David watch

Bathsheba? How long did it take King Solomon to surrender to his many concubines? How long does it take for a man to watch another man's wife until he begins to subtly flirt with her? How long does it take for a man to become so discontent with his wife that he plans to take another man's wife? It is a slow process that begins with a willing, unprotected heart.

The tragedy is that the numbers of moral failures and acts of personal impurity are far greater than we can ever know because of the many ways churches deal with issue. Many churches simply release the person and do nothing, hoping he'll change in the next church. Some churches never confront. Some churches remove the minister but on spurious charges for fear of a lawsuit. Many churches call adultery improper behavior; some call addiction to pornography "his little issue" (!), or they say nothing at all. God calls it sin, and the church suffers because of our impurity and tolerance of sin. The consequence of this sin is devastating on the church and families involved.

The solution begins with personal confession—confession that genuinely allows God to forgive and cleanse, not just lip service. Hopefully this occurs at salvation when the person becomes a new creature and at any time that the person allows sin to separate him from God. Hopefully there is a forsaking of what was one way prior to Christ, and now in Christ, they are in every way pure and holy. It is the hatred of sin and the impurity that entangles our hearts. True confession does not allow false fences of religion to be erected at the expense of true forgiveness. I have met many religious folks who develop very stringent systems (fences) to keep them from sinning, but they always fail! Making resolutions won't work, nor will stubborn determinism. But confession that leads one to forsake or never start is where it begins for all who are successful.

> I have met many religious folks who develop very stringent systems (fences) to keep them from sinning, but they always fail!

The second step is being honest with oneself in recognizing the potential for failure and our desperate need to be dependent on Christ. As a result, we align our lives to obedience of the Word of God and submit to the power of the Holy Spirit to have control over us. This doesn't just happen. It happens when it is my will and desire to submit to His will. It happens when I choose to obey the Word. It happens when I daily say yes to His forgiveness and allow Him to control me. This must become my life, not just a rabbit's foot I rub on occasion for good luck. Purity happens when I recognize I can fail, but surrender to His will and word. I must daily be in the Word of God. My day must begin in the Word, and it must be the Word from which I find the guidance and direction of God. Daily ingesting the Word also requires daily meditating on the Word in order that it will bring understanding and clarity to my life. If I am truly thinking about what God has said to me through His Word, I must also be intentional about hiding it in my heart so that I won't sin against my Lord. Only as I allow God's Word to become a daily part of my life will I understand what it means to have God's Word dwell in me richly. I must practice hearing, reading studying, memorizing and meditating on God's Word if I am to walk in the purity and holiness he has called me.

> The failure among pastors is many times the direct result of their pride and resulting isolation from accountability and relationships.

The third step is ongoing prayer. This again includes regular confession and the forsaking of anything that might lead me down a path of impurity. Prayer is how we start our day; it is how we walk through the day, talking to the Lord about the day. Prayer is our communication with Him just as He communicates with us through His Word. Prayer is praise, intercession and thanksgiving. I had a friend many years ago promise to pray for me every time he was tempted, and I committed to pray for him when I was tempted. It was amazing how God was able to take my mind off the temptation and focus it on the need and circumstance of my friend. Prayer allows me the opportunity to respond to Him about what He has said to me in His Word. It allows me to apply the Word in faith as I talk to my Father. Prayer begins with confession and is critical to our walk of purity.

The fourth choice or step is to find accountability among your friends in Christ. You can't do this alone. You can perhaps make it for a while, but eventually there will be a collapse. Being a pastor or minister does not exempt you. The failure among pastors is many times the direct result of their pride and resulting isolation from accountability and relationships. The Christian faith is a faith meant to be lived out in the context of community; no exceptions! I am not talking about whining sessions or therapy groups. I am talking about friends that know you and speak truth to you, and because they love you, you will listen to them. The kind of relationships I am talking about won't allow you to blow smoke or walk a con. They know if you are holding out. They pursue you. I have had friends that were beginning to stumble down the road of impurity, and the first thing they avoided was their true friends. They were always too busy (when in reality they were sinning). To walk in purity is to hold ourselves in godly relationships.

Another aspect of this is to allow older brothers to have access to our lives. Though I think the concept of mentoring is extremely needful, it has become almost meaningless in today's vernacular. But regardless of what the world is devolving down to, we all need mentors, persons of godly wisdom that can challenge us and correct us. This is what the community of believers is supposed to look like. This is what we need if we are to walk in purity.

You only have one testimony. Will you guard your testimony? Will you walk in purity and holiness? When you became a Christian you were declared holy, but the process of sanctification necessitates our obedience and commitment to walk in a way that insures our purity.

Blessed are the pure in heart for they shall see God.   Matthew 5:8

Being Black and White in a Gray World: Is There Such a Thing as Truth? {12}

Sanctify them by the truth; your word is truth.   John 17:17 (NIV)

Jesus said to him, "I am the way, and the truth, and the life; no one comes to the Father, but by me."   John 14:6

Every word of God proves true; he is a shield to those who take refuge in him. Do not add to his words, lest he rebuke you, and you be found a liar.   Proverbs 30:5-6

Have you ever listened to the evening news and wondered what is going on? Have you had a conversation with someone who was struggling with something that seemed so very clear to you that you couldn't understand their struggle? With the insanity of our political environment to the global warning debate, it seems that very few see things in black and white any more. The more our politicians speak the more certain it becomes that they are many times clueless or just purposely vague. Vague is a good word describing the gray matter of our current scenario. Ambiguity would also fit or perhaps wavering. It just seems that the more a person seems to have answers the more they seem to waffle about the specifics. Waffle would be another good word, not the pastry type of waffle, but rather referring to one who is wishy-washy about most everything.

In my humble opinion we live in a very gray world. People are afraid, it seems, to say anything that would perhaps be construed as absolute, black and white or without flexibility for reinterpretation. If someone says something with conviction and confidence, there tends to be the shock of something being judged. In this day of over used political correctness, we have lost the courage to have conviction or see things for what they are. Some who even see black and white will pretend only to see gray to avoid the reaction or ridicule it brings. We can only be black and white about the things we aren't sure of. We have become a nation of persons who take great pride in the knowledge that we aren't sure. The true loser is truth. We can't tolerate something that purports itself to be absolutely true, so we don't.

Black and white people are many times accused of being simple minded, or thought to not be able to grasp the complicated nature of the issues. Our schools and universities embrace uncertainty and only tend to judge and attack those who are certain and clear. Seeing in black and white does not excuse ignorance or stupidity. Being black and white isn't without its faults. Racism is a product of persons who saw in black and white, but only proved the critics correct, as they were stupid and rejected truth. Being black and white doesn't mean my way or the highway, but it can mean "I" see the highway! Being black and white doesn't mean a person can't see all the issues; it means that a person sees through the smoke and mirrors and gets to the heart of the issue. Being black and white causes one to not get lost on the periphery of issues because they are tethered to a greater truth.

> Being black and white causes one to not get lost in the periphery of issues because they are tethered to a greater truth.

So before I get too far, I apologize to all of my gray-area friends, not for my simplicity or clarity, but I apologize, or should I say I am sorry that you just don't get it! I am sorry that principles are hard for you to grasp, let alone stand on. I am truly sorry that your world has to be so complex and disjointed, because in many cases it doesn't have to be. I am sorry that you vacillate in the area of absolute truth.

Again, seeing things in black and white terms and holding to absolute truth doesn't negate the complexity of many issues, but it allows principled wisdom to be called upon to bring clarity. It exposes values that are of an absolute nature and not as transient and relative as our culture tends to embrace. What constitutes truth?

To those who see only in terms of gray, this is a difficult question which is almost impossible to answer. The tragedy of this uncertainty is found among those who would consider themselves followers of Jesus Christ. These confessors believe in Jesus as Savior but don't want to hurt the feelings of Mormons, Jehovah Witnesses, Scientologists, or any other spurious cult. They can with clarity say Jesus is the way, but since He is love, He will obviously make provision for these other groups. They can with a clear conscience maintain that the Bible is God's inspired Word while maintaining that the Koran, the book of Mormon and others may also have their place. They are big about not judging, unless of course they encounter someone who doesn't register on their "tolerance meter," and then it is OK to

> For something to be absolutely true it means that there will never be a time when the statement will not be true.

be caustically judgmental. So here is the problem for so-called evangelical Christians: is the Bible absolutely true, and more importantly, is Jesus the truth; is He truly the way and the life? I say more importantly because I don't believe that the Bible is part of the Trinity.

What do we do with John 14:6? Jesus speaking says, "I am the way, and the truth, and the life, no one comes to the father, but by me." What do we do with John 17:17? Again Jesus speaking, "Sanctify them in the truth; thy word is truth." Pilate asked the question that is all too often asked today, "What is truth?" Because our culture has such an aversion to something being absolute with no room for dissension, we struggle with truth outside of a relativistic context. When we say something is true, what do we mean? First, it means that something is objectively accurate without any mixture of error. In this context it doesn't assume that something is absolutely true.

Let me explain. In the days of Jesus, a person could say in truth, that men could not fly. It was true in the context. Man could not fly, and it was not even fathomable. It would have been just as accurate to say man cannot fly to the moon. In the context of the day it was true, but these statements would not be considered absolutely true. For something to be absolutely true it means that there will never be a time when the statement will not be true. Second, in the case of Jesus and His Word, truth is not just accurate but absolute. The difference again, is that there will never be a time regardless of context that it is not true. The law of gravity is binding on earth but men can now fly. There are truths that are bound in a particular context but when removed from the stated context become false. Jesus and His Word is absolute. He is always and absolutely true. He is the Son of God on Mars and Earth; He is the resurrected Lord in all quadrants of the universe. He is part of the Holy Trinity throughout what is called time. He is absolutely true, and His Word is absolutely true without error.

Here is the rub. To hold something as absolutely true requires an element called faith, not to verify the fact of the truth, but rather to see it. As an evangelical Christian, I hold to the historical verifiable resurrection of Jesus Christ. I hold it as an absolute fact, but faith is required. The skeptic who denies the reality of an absolute truth rejects the element of faith that is required to see, especially where it is found in a spiritual or theological context. I am utterly shocked and amazed at those who reject spiritual fact in the name of science.

A number of years ago I was on a flight from Denver to San Francisco. I found myself seated next to a gentleman who told me he had fought with Britain in the Falkland Island war against Argentina. His story was extremely interesting, if not a tad bit unbelievable (he seemed rather young). We conversed for quite a while. When I shared my journey of coming to believe in Christ as my savior, he shared with me that he was an agnostic. He confirmed this by maintaining that if there was a superior being, it could not be known or identified. He did state that he believed in science. As we continued our dialogue for a while, he began to tell me of all he maintained about the cosmos, its origins and the science used to substantiate his belief system. His dishonesty (totally unaware) was exposed in what he believed to be factual concerning the origins of

> To hold something as absolutely true requires an element called faith, not to verify the fact of the truth, but rather to see it.

the universe. He called it science when in reality it was a gargantuan leap of blind faith.

The science he purported to hold barely qualified as theory, yet he held to his propositions without reservation. In fact one of the biggest deceptions of our day is the science of origins; i.e., evolution that presents a theory so bizarre it is more sci-fi than reliable data. The truth is this elaborate scheme is basically the cover for denying the existence of God, an absolute being who created. They maintain chaos over order and probabilities so astronomically improbable that it begs for reason.

But, back to my friend on the plane. As we landed and were de-boarding the jet he thanked me for our conversation. I told him I admired his zeal but found it unfortunate that someone so bright would give himself to a life position that demanded so much blind faith—something I would not do. He would categorically reject the tenets of Christianity as mere fiction while holding as absolute truth the theories of something unimaginable.

The aforementioned account is all too common today. Society rejects the notion of something being absolutely true, particularly if it is in the arena of theology, but has no problem holding science to be absolute in its presentation of God-less theory. So when we speak of something being true, we are usually met with skepticism. Science has rendered truth as unacceptable outside of its own ever-evolving perameters. Science truly opened the door to chaos when it imposed itself as the new deity, the new absolute.

On the other side of the spectrum are those who maintain a trite puppy love type of understanding of truth. They maintain something to be true, for the moment, as long as they feel it is true. From this line of thought has emerged the idea of something being true for some but not necessarily for others. A 16 year old boy is truly in love for life with his girlfriend. He is willing to die for her, fight for her, but he really just wants to be physically intimate with her. To many this is truly love, truth in its purest most absolute form, until they break up and the emotional rollercoaster ride begins again, but it is all true.

Of course, this barely constitutes anything related to something being absolutely true. But yet it does, in that some have reduced truth to feeling, emotion and simple reflective assent. Truth becomes random and in constant motion. Faith is relegated to the same feeling and emotive quality. This model of faith has little to do with historical Christianity which maintains a faith above the limits of mere feeling and emotion.

Many years ago, Campus Crusade for Christ developed the gospel tract called the Four Spiritual Laws. Towards the back of the little tract is a diagram of a train. Fact is the engine, Faith the middle car and Feeling the caboose. Our belief system really is like the train. Feelings can't pull the train, nor can faith if it is without the substance of fact. We who are evangelical Christians are those who believe in the historically verifiable events of the Bible as propositional objective truth. Not truth for a certain context, but an absolute truth. The incarnation (God becoming flesh in Jesus), the crucifixion, and the bodily resurrection are held to be irrefutable absolute facts. We hold as absolute truth the fact that our God created out of nothing all that is now known, and what He didn't, God gave His creation (humankind) the minds to do—i.e., jets, automobiles, space shuttles, and so forth. He even allows us the capability to doubt and even reject Him!

> The incarnation (God becoming flesh in Jesus), the crucifixion, and the bodily resurrection are held to be irrefutable absolute facts.

So here it is. We either believe that the Scriptures are absolutely true in their presentation of God, or they are not. Some might be like Karl Barth who maintained the Bible contained the word of God but of itself was not God's Word. In this thinking, truth becomes subjective rather than objective. His contemporary Rudolph Bultman maintained the need to de-mythologize the Bible to find the true word. These views clearly accentuate the problem as to what is meant by something being absolutely true. Barth and Bultman would not hold the Scriptures known as the Bible to be absolutely true. For the black and white mind, it either is or it isn't. It is either truth, or it is false. Jesus was the way, the truth, and the life, or He was a fake and a liar. As C.S. Lewis proposed, Jesus was either Lord, or He was a liar or a lunatic.

Faith simply reveals what we see to be true. The Scientologist sees Ron L. Hubbard as a speaker of truth; the Muslim world sees Mohammad as the true guide to Allah; the Mormons hold to the teaching of Smith and Young as necessary to find truth. It takes a huge leap of faith to believe the tenets of their claims just like that of the chaos theories of some scientists. The problem with such groups is the absolute lack of verifiable fact. I asked a couple of Mormon elders why it was so hard for their organization to be honest. They will not allow any scrutiny of the documents they profess to hold that validate their claims. This very attitude makes substantive faith impossible. It simply is a religious form of blind faith, not faith based on fact.

Is our faith rooted in science, feeling, religion, or fact? The Christian faith as taught in the Bible is the most exclusive. Even though it teaches God's love for all persons, it is clear in its presentation of the narrow way as the only way. This makes it a hard pill to swallow for those who see gray. A gray world is a tolerant world that embraces all avenues of searching for anything perceived as truth. Christianity loves all searchers but warns that all ways except the way of Christ are dead ends with consequences that are eternally bad for the holder.

> Living life without absolutes is like riding a rollercoaster without railing or guards.

Truth is a perplexing dilemma. It either is or it isn't. If Jesus is who the Scriptures portray Him to be, He is the absolute truth of God and is in fact God. This is a huge problem for those who like options or multiple correct answers. To a black and white believer it makes sense and brings clarity. To those caught up in gray, the absolute nature of Christ and even the Bible are rather problematic to say the least. The very nature of something being absolutely true means that anything else is absolutely wrong! If something is absolutely true, then it isn't mean-spirited or intolerant to reveal its opposite as indeed absolutely false. Absolute truth is what it is, and this truth brings clarity to life and clarity of purpose. Living life without absolutes is like riding a rollercoaster without railing or guards. Without absolute truth, life is a rudderless ship adrift in the middle of the ocean. One's ability to make value judgments or determine right from wrong is now based on nothing more than feeling or opinion. Absolute truth brings absolute clarity to an absolutely confused world.

Ethics: What We Do and Say Matters

Whatever your task, work heartily, as serving the Lord and not men.

Colossians 3:23

Instead, speaking the truth in love, we will in all things grow up into him who is the Head, that is, Christ.   Ephesians 4:15 (NIV)

And whatever you do, in word or deed, do everything in the name of the Lord Jesus.   Colossians 3:17a

The good man brings good things out of the good stored up in his heart, and the evil man brings evil things out of the evil stored up in his heart. For out of the overflow of his heart his mouth speaks.

Luke 6:45 (NIV)

Ethics are the standards of spiritual and moral values on which a ministry is built. Our ethics reveal our character and our integrity. In the service of Christ this is one area—along with moral purity—that must be above reproach and criticism. Our work habits, our truthfulness in speech, our personal righteous are all demonstrations of our ethics. Over the many years of serving in the context of church ministry, I have had the privilege of meeting many persons who truly were men of integrity and honor. Their work and speech ethic were impeccable. Tragically, I have also met men and women along the way who served in leadership capacities, whose work and speech ethic revealed character flaws. I think of a pastor with whom I once worked. He would regularly wish to confide in me things concerning other people, but he would always end his statement with, "If you tell anyone I said this, I'll deny every word!" That statement always concerned me, not because I would repeat it, but because the man had no conscience about lying about it! This particular pastor went on to serve in a denominational capacity. I hope he is an exception to the rule, but I fear his type may be all too prominent.

Does it matter how we work, and by this I mean the quality and quantity of our work? Does it matter that I work a full load if I am full-time? What does it say about me if I constantly cut corners and take breaks and cheat my church of the time they expect or even deserve from me? I have worked with numerous persons who were at their best, sluggards. They developed the attitude that they were underpaid and therefore they were free from any obligation of faithful, productive work. They hid behind family, education, and inadequate pay, but were all the same, sluggards. If you are called to a full-time position, what does that mean? Does it mean give them (the church) only what you feel they are paying you? Does it mean you only do for them what you perceive they are willing to do for you? If I accept a position in ministry and am aware of the pay and expectations, and I accept the position as posted, I have but one ethical position—to do that which I agreed to do. Anything less is the testimony of a lazy thief. Lazy, because I am revealing a sluggard's attitude; thief because I am robbing from them what I agreed to do for them—and both are inexcusable attitudes!

> I have worked with numerous persons who were at their best, sluggards.

Another dangerous game we play that reveals our work ethic and character is the comparison game. When I begin to compare myself to others and use my conclusions as justification for bad behavior, I have been defeated by pride. Never forget that God hates pride! Comparisons are rooted in dissatisfaction based on assumptions such as, "I am not appreciated;" "I work harder than any one else;" "I am not paid enough for what they expect;" "I am more qualified than my boss;" "I work harder than the full-time people," and on and on! Comparisons are the enemy of contentment and God has commanded us to be content.

Paul put it well in Philippians 4:11, where he states, "Not that I complain of want; for I have learned, in whatever state I am, to be content." One's focus is what makes this a reality. If I am looking at my circumstances I will rarely be content, and the comparisons might run wild. If my focus is on Christ and I remember why I do what I do, it puts things in an eternal rather than temporal perspective. Why do we do what we do? Do we do it for recognition and the accolades of men? Consider the following verse, "Am I seeking the favor of men, or of God? Or am I trying to please men? If I were still pleasing men, I should not be a servant of Christ" (Galatians1:10). The discontented of heart will rarely, if ever, do their job for the glory of God, and they will never ever be satisfied or free from the trap of comparisons. Comparisons will always rob us of the joy God would have us know. Contentment reveals much about our personal ethic and character.

Our ethics are all exposed at the point of small things. How well do I do the seemingly insignificant? How faithful am I when I feel the job is below me? Do I have integrity in the little things? In the parable of the talents, much is said about the character of the three servants without being said. If we were the players in the story, which of the three would we be most like? Are we working for an audience of *One* or for the applause of men? Would words like steadfast and immovable be characteristic of my work ethic? Would we be considered faithful or faithless? I have worked with men who you always knew would always do a job poorly, if at all. I remember in seminary, where I worked as a janitor, I was cleaning a restroom one day, thinking to myself that as a college graduate I was really going places cleaning toilets! I was feeling above the job. God spoke to me that day (not audibly!) and reminded me that until I was faithful in the cleaning of porcelain I would have nothing to say to anyone, particularly from the pulpit. My attitude changed that day and I purposed to be the best janitor I could be for *His* glory! You see our work ethic ought to be for His glory and ought to reveal His character in us! Consider 1 Corinthians 10:31b, "whatever you do, do all to the glory of God."

Another critical area of our ethics is found in the matter of our speech, most pointedly in the issue of speaking the truth. In a post-modern world truth is perceived as relative and personal. We however, as God's servants, must allow no such concessions. Over the thirty-five years I have served in churches I have regularly heard things regarding ministers, such as, "he just exaggerates a lot," or "he tends to embellish a little," or "we never put too much stock in what he says, he doesn't mean to lie," and on and on. These types of references are tragic. What is being said, in essence, is that these men lie! They do not speak the truth. Their word doesn't mean much. What a tragedy! What an embarrassment to the cause of Christ when the spokesmen for Christ are not to be believed. All too often we have more in common with the lying prophets that Isaiah and Jeremiah confronted, rather than the true prophets of God themselves. We ought to be people who are known by the character of our speech, the integrity of our words and not the dishonesty of our lips.

Consider Proverbs 19:1, "Better is a poor man who walks in his integrity than a man who is perverse in his speech and is a fool." In a time of growing moral and ethical failure in our political leaders, and increasingly in our spiritual leaders, we must be all the more diligent in the area of our character, integrity and ethics. What I say and how I say it says volumes about the condition of my heart and exposes the nature of my personal ethic. If I find it easy to lie, deceive, or even cheat, and if I find it easier to exaggerate than to speak truth, then I have a heart issue. I remember an incident years ago in another city where we were having a city-wide crusade with a well known evangelist. I was in charge of counseling and decisions. At the end of the crusade we had seen almost 500 people give their lives to Jesus Christ as Lord and Savior. I turned the number of conversions over to our crusade coordinator. In our next state denominational paper I was shocked to see that over 1,500 people had been converted. I immediately contacted the coordinator who told me that he and the evangelist had determined that our numbers were too conservative and that we had probably missed a few people. A few people! They added 1,000 people to the numbers! What was evident to me was that the reputation of the evangelist was more important than the truth. The cold reality is that it did say volumes about the evangelist and those who collaborated with his lie.

All involved showed a huge lack of character, and their ethics were revealed for what they were—dishonest! If it is this easy to lie in a denominational newspaper, how easy is it to lie to one's family or church? How easy is it to make promises with absolutely no intention of keeping them?

Our ethics ought to be derived from the Word of God and spring from our relationship with Christ. We ought to be men and women who in every way demonstrate spiritual transformation rather than worldly conformity. I expect those without Christ to fix the numbers, alter the bottom line, but never the ministers of Christ. I am not surprised when a politician might lie or try to cover up a bigger lie, but it should never be true of us. We must be a people who do what we say, mean what we say, and say that which is the truth. There is never an appropriate time to lie. We are called to always speak truth. Our ethics should dictate our Godly behavior and truthful speech. We should, plain and simply, be people whose word is their bond.

> We must be persons whose work ethic is above reproach and whose speech is without guile.

In a world of compromise and ethical surrender we must be relentless in our stand for truth and integrity. We must be persons whose work ethic is above reproach and whose speech is without guile. Tragically, I have in my limited experience seen far to many who were anything but ethical either in speech or behavior. Too many pastors preach but do not practice. Too many are known for their words, but their words aren't known for their truthfulness. It is to our shame that this is true. If we hold the Bible to be God's perfect Word, if we maintain that we are a new creature in Christ, if we testify to God's transforming power, we must flesh out an ethical life that is rooted in the truth of Christ.

I have served with those who felt they were grossly underpaid and therefore would only work as hard as they felt was "fitting" for their pay. If they had integrity, they should have resigned or repented. Instead, they almost always have to be removed. I have worked with far too many ministers who rarely spoke the truth, rarely came clean, and almost never owned up to their deceit. Eventually, they have all fallen to the wayside. Ironically they blame everyone but themselves. They have never accepted the fact that they were at best, lazy and many, at their worst, plain and simply, liars. Far too many of them still live in the lie, the lie of denial of personal responsibility! I am not suggesting that a pastor can't tell a story or a joke or at times embellish a story, if they acknowledge what they are doing and always clarify what they have done. But we all know the difference.

Do you keep your promises even to your own hurt? Do you do what you say without excuse and accept responsibility when you don't. We must be persons whose work ethic is impeccable and speech truthful. We must be a people who are not marginalized by compromise and the surrender of values. Our ethics reveal our character, which reveals our values, which are born out of our faith. So the bottom line is, how is your faith doing? Remember that out of the abundance of our hearts our mouths speak. It is also equally true to say that out of the abundance of our hearts we act! If you were to ask people who watch your life closely, how would they describe your work ethic? What would they say about your speech? Would you be known for your hard and diligent work? Would you be known as one who speaks truth and is without question reliable and dependable?

It should be obvious that our ethics are showing for good or bad. What are your ethics revealing about you? What would your wife or kids say about your ethics? I am reminded of an old poem I read in a Navigator Bible study: "You are writing a gospel, a chapter each day, by things that you do and the words that you say, people read what you write, distorted or true, what is the gospel according to you?"

It needs to be remembered that our ethics are showing. Our ethics reveal our character, and one of the most revealing times our ethics are on display is when no one is watching. What are they saying about you? Do your words honor God with truth? Regardless of one's eschatology, we all agree that we will all stand before God and give an accounting for our lives. If your life came to an end this very day, what would your record of accounts say about you? May it be true of us that we fleshed out our biblical ethics with holy sincerity and godly integrity!

Whatever Happened to Our Convictions? {14}

"King Agrippa, do you believe the prophets? I know that you believe."
And Agrippa said to Paul, "In a short time you think to make me a
Christian!" And Paul said, "Whether short or long, I would to God that
not only you but also all who hear me this day might become such as
I am—except for these chains." Acts 26:27-29

If ethics reveal character, convictions reveal our values and beliefs. I have
met people who were convicted about drinking, dancing, dating, money,
work, church, family, new and old cars, and the list could go on forever.
Most of what people are convicted about has either been inherited from
other sources or many times, from our own guilt. How many have argued
against dancing because that is how they were raised, not because they
had a genuine biblical conviction. How many have a conviction because
they got caught and the guilt led to an emotional conviction? Picture the
husband who embraces the wife by his side affirming his love and devotion
after his affair has been exposed. Now that is a picture of conviction. *Not!*
By definition, a conviction is (for our purpose) something that is strongly
believed to be true and subsequently alters, shapes and determines one's
belief and behavior.

In the mid 1930s thousands of young Germans marched with
conviction in the belief that the Third Reich was the rightful world rule
of Germany, and that they were a vastly superior people group. Many
people died to prove their conviction. Lenin, Stalin, Mao, Castro, Che
and many others were convicted that communism was the true utopian
way and consequently literally millions were killed to prove it. Our own

country was founded by those with strong convictions about personal freedoms, even if they were not extended to all persons. Our bloodiest war was between brothers equally convicted about the issues of freedom as it related to slavery and the role of the federal government. The Democrats are just as convicted as the Republicans, and they each prove it with their abundant verbiage, countless promises, and attacks against the other side. Napoleon was convicted he was to rule the world, but between Russian winters and Waterloo he lost thousands of troops to be proven wrong. The list can go on and on giving illustration after illustration of people with deep convictions.

Even among Christians the Word is thrown around frequently and with great emotion. Catholics were convicted to persecute and eradicate Luther; Calvin was convicted to kill Anabaptists and rid the world of Arminius. For hundreds of years the crusaders were convicted that the Muslims should be destroyed, particularly in Jerusalem. The Muslims still remember how the crusaders acted (very similar to how they acted!). They still, to this day, cite the crusades as fire for their conviction that the "Western Satan" deserves death. The pages of history are filled with people who lived and died with conviction and much of it has not been good.

> A conviction is something that is strongly believed to be true and subsequently alters, shapes and determines one's belief and behavior.

Consider what I believe to be examples worthy of imitation. Paul was convicted not to take John Mark on the second missionary journey. Barnabas was equally convicted that he should go. Paul was convicted to go Macedonia. Paul was convicted to go to Jerusalem even in the face of imprisonment. Paul was convicted to go to Rome to see Caesar, even if it would mean his death! Paul is a model of a man of Godly convictions. His life direction appears to be the result of his convictions. He was the apostle to the gentile world out of personal conviction. He was convicted to strongly oppose any Jewish additions to the Christian gospel. Paul's life was a testimony of man who lived and died by his convictions. His convictions led him down a path that few would tread today. Why? Our conviction ought to spring from a transforming belief in what the Word of God says.

We ought to be as convicted about our faith as was Paul. Why are the Jim Elliots (one of five men willing to risk life itself to reach a tribe of known killers with the gospel of Christ) of this world so seemingly rare? We are convicted about expositional preaching, Calvinism, denominationalism, strategies, etc., but these things have so little to do with what motivated and consumed Paul. We have become masters of holy business, but not of God's business. I can hear someone arguing that expositional preaching is God's primary business or that Calvinism is God's way. Dear friend, expositional preaching is a method, and methods are many and ever changing. Calvinism is a man-created system of belief rooted in philosophical fatalism. It even bears his name.

But where are the convictions about living as Jesus did? We teach taking up our crosses but always have our resumes circulating in case "God" has a bigger church with a bigger paycheck somewhere out there. We preach self-denial and then go get in our new Lexus. We spend hours dissecting Greek verbs, but won't go talk to our neighbor. We preach the infallibility of Scripture and choose to discriminate against certain people groups. We say that the Scriptures are perfect, without error (and they are!) and then live such hypocritical lives that no one is interested in what we have to say. We have perfected the art of Pharisaism. By this I mean we have compartmentalized our belief from our behavior. Our convictions are about things that have little or nothing to do with the Kingdom of God. What ought we be convicted about? What shaped Paul and motivated him with such conviction? Shouldn't our passion for Christ and His Word be as foundational for us as it was for Paul?

> Our conviction ought to spring from a transforming belief in what the Word of God says.

We ought to be convicted about the righteousness of God based on faith in Christ. We ought to be convicted by obedience that allows us to experience and know the presence of Christ. We ought to be convicted about grace. We ought to have strong conviction about answered prayer and the will of God. We should have strong conviction regarding the love of God in Christ and the power of forgiveness. We ought to have strong convictions regarding the fact that God is faithful and does not abandon or forsake us. These are just a few of the doctrinal positions one ought to be strongly convicted about. The tragic reality is that we more often loudly verbalize convictions concerning things like preferred forms of worship, which Bible is used, which system of belief one adheres to, which position of eschatology one espouses and so forth. These are worthy of discussion and even debate, but they are not central to anything even vaguely associated with expanding the Kingdom of God or the fulfillment of the Great Commission, except in a negative way.

Let me explain. I just returned from a trip to Africa, where I spent an extended period of time with a most extraordinary man named Ade. He was educated in Great Britain and had been professor at one of the universities of his home country before God got his attention. He has given up everything to make disciples and start churches in the remote villages in the Muslim areas of his country, in places where no Christian witness existed. God has given life to 20-plus churches and entire villages have come to the saving knowledge of Jesus Christ. I personally saw the results of God's work in villages we stayed in. Ade is like an old circuit rider. Most of the pastors can't read or write, but they have been powerfully transformed by Christ. The churches they lead give evidence of the life, presence and power of Christ, even without knowledge of the Greek or Hebrew. I contrast this with a group of pastors who had been in the same country at the same time, staying in the city and teaching expositional preaching. One is involved in expanding the Kingdom of God; the others were simply teaching a method (albeit a very good one!). One is a testimony of convictions given to principles, the other convictions given to methodology, and there is an eternal difference.

I have personal convictions, such as the total abstinence from any form of alcohol. I realize that the Bible doesn't say one can't drink, and I seriously doubt that Jesus used grape juice at the Last Supper, but that doesn't mean one should drink. My conviction stems from a few corollary beliefs.

First, I believe that God calls us to be wise, and the use of alcohol opens the possibility for really stupid behavior and speech. It also has the potential for destructive addiction. I have never known an alcoholic who planned on being one! It also is an acute stumbling block for many who have suffered from its addictive power, and for me to use it would be a slap in their face.

On a very personal note, I have seen far too closely the damage of alcohol. My wife's family was devastated by alcoholism; my best high school buddies died in alcohol related accidents; my own family has been hit hard by the destructive nature of alcohol abuse. I am aware that over 50% of all fatalities on our highways are alcohol related, most crimes are alcohol related and on and on. If wisdom is important, I feel that the consumption of alcoholic beverages would be incredibly foolish and extremely unwise. For me, as James 4:17 says, "to know to do good and not do it is sin." So my personal conviction is abstinence! My conviction is based on my understanding of biblical teaching, cultural relevance, medical fact, reality and personal experience.

I have other personal convictions that are similar in their development and application for my life. I strongly advocate my own convictions but realize another Christian might disagree based on a different process of judgment. I would still, by conviction, disagree with them. Because these are personal convictions for me, fellowship is not necessarily an issue, though there might have to be some heavy discussion. This is very different from my conviction that Jesus is the only way, truth and life when encountering someone who sees many possibilities of salvation. My conviction is a "line in the sand" that will affect my relationship with them. I cannot fellowship with a person who denies that Jesus is the resurrected Son of God. I cannot appreciate or tolerate a belief system that alters or manipulates the Trinity. I cannot respect a belief system that adds to the teachings of the Bible, let alone fellowship with those who alter its message. I can, however, love them, be friendly to them, and pray that

> I strongly advocate my own convictions but realize another Christian might disagree based on a different process of judgment.

someday they would come to Jesus Christ as their Savior and Lord. They aren't my enemies; they are my mission field.

Will we prove to be men and women convicted about truth and honesty? Will we be convicted about moral purity and ethical dignity? Will we prove to be men who know the difference between our opinions and God's inerrant truth? Our convictions must be based on the truth and the truth is the Word of God.

Growing up, I heard sermons that expressed the preacher's convictions. Convictions against dancing, smoking, drinking, cards, movies, shorts, short dresses, long hair, shaved heads, piercing, tattoo's, holding hands, dating, kissing, music, on and on. I am sure that most of these sermons were rooted in sincerity, but sometimes what was called a conviction was nothing more than a personal vendetta against change or a fear of something new. Sometimes the apparent conviction was based on poor interpretation of Scriptures. Sometimes it was based on a perceived moral Pandora's Box, a fear of the unknown. Sometimes it was about control. I personally agree with many of the things I have heard, but not all and most assuredly, I understand that much of this is my opinion and my own fence rather than a conviction based on the teaching of Scripture in context.

May we prove to be persons with deep biblical convictions that then give birth to other personal convictions that are consistent with our faith. May we stand against the things Jesus stood against. We must fight the temptation to stand as the Pharisees, who were convinced that they were so right, but they were consistently wrong. For example, they were correct to preach resting on the Sabbath but wrong to develop intricate rules to enforce its observance. We live in a time when convictions are fluid and relative. It must not be so among us. We must be people of deep biblical convictions who truly show what righteous holy living is, not what it isn't.

Dealing with Crisis

Consider it pure joy, my brothers, whenever you face trials of many
kinds, because you know that the testing of your faith develops
perseverance. Perseverance must finish its work so that you may be
mature and complete, not lacking anything.   James 1:2-4 (NIV)

He is like a man building a house, who dug deep, and laid the foundation upon rock; and when a flood arose, the stream broke against that
house, and could not shake it, because it had been well built.
                                                              Luke 6:48

My persecutions, my sufferings, what befell me at Antioch, at Iconium,
and at Lystra, what persecutions I endured; yet from them all the
Lord rescued me. Indeed all who desire to live a godly life will be
persecuted.   2 Timothy 3:11-12

Beloved, do not be surprised at the fiery ordeal which comes upon you
to prove you, as though something strange were happening to you.
But rejoice in so far as you share Christ's sufferings, that you may also
rejoice and be glad when his glory is revealed.   1 Peter 4:12-13

In this you rejoice, though now for a little while you may have to suffer
various trials, so that the genuineness of your faith, more precious than
gold which though perishable is tested by fire, may redound to praise
and glory and honor at the revelation of Jesus Christ.
                                                           1 Peter 1:6-7

Crisis, trials, life storms or whatever you may choose to call them will occur, whether we like it or not. We can't plan when they will come, yet we can anticipate them. They will never be a comfortable fit, nor will we ever acquire a taste for them. In fact most of us, if we are normal, will always look for ways to avoid them. After all who likes pain, sorrow, loss, or the feelings of desperation? Some whole belief systems have in the name of faith denied their very existence. Some call all crisis the tool of the devil and his demons. Some just surrender to what they perceive as the inevitable sea of trials and see it as their plight in life, i.e. the Charlie Brown syndrome.

> **The presence of storms has nothing to do with one's faith or lack thereof, but it has everything to do with living in a fallen world.**

But for most of us we understand that life storms will come, though sometimes we forget that they will. None of us like these times, but we should learn to expect them and see them as tools that in the hands of God can work for our good. This is exactly what Romans 8:28 is referring to. "We know that in everything God works for good, with those who love him, who are called according to his purpose." Paul isn't saying that all things are good. He isn't promising a bed of roses. He simply says that God is always at work and in all circumstances for those who love Him and will work every situation for their ultimate good.

I need to qualify that I am not talking about the storms that come into our lives because of our stupidity or sin. It is like the guy who smokes for 40 years and then is diagnosed with terminal lung cancer and wonders why God has allowed this! Or consider the man who always drives recklessly and dangerously fast. When the inevitable wreck occurs, and a family member is killed or seriously injured, they wonder why God did this to them. This is like playing with a loaded gun and then wondering why it went off in my hand. Reckless living or sinful indulgence will always have a consequence, and this is not what God wanted, but what we chose. Storms of life don't need assistance or help, and no one is immune from them.

Some of my Charismatic brethren see every negative life storm as an attack of the devil. They seek deliverance, healing, or try to "cast it out," but it remains, because it has nothing to do with what they think. It is a lesson of life, one that can either reveal the working of God for our growth, or it is one that results in the diminishing of our faith, and there is nothing gained but bitterness. They can claim faith or speak some spurious word from God, but the storm will come and run its course. Will they learn its lesson, or will they need to go back to school? This is what is in the balance.

The presence of storms has nothing to do with one's faith or lack thereof, but it has everything to do with living in a fallen world. My brothers can deny them or pray against them, but it isn't the devil who sends them. If we were speaking of temptations, we could agree, but life storms, the crisis that we all will face, is a different matter. I am quite sure that those of the Charismatic persuasion will die of cancer, heart disease, birth defects, car wrecks or other causes in the same numbers and ratios as that of Baptist, Evangelical Free and even Catholics. It is about life, not sin, not the devil, not some demon. I am not saying that the devil can't bring evil to our door, but I am saying that much of what the Charismatic calls evil is simply life in a fallen world, and God will work it for good if we allow Him to do so.

I remember the Sunday before my youngest son was scheduled to have reconstructive heart surgery in December of 1980. We had asked God to heal him. My wife even took him to be prayed over by a famous "healer" in Tulsa, Oklahoma. But here we were on the eve of his surgery, and the crisis was still at hand. I remember, when Josh was born, how I was shocked! Bad things weren't supposed to happen to me. I led people to Christ, I memorized Scripture, I tithed. I did all the right things. I didn't smoke or drink or anything that would be a cause of this "evil" thing. I was not even Charismatic, but somehow had bought into a belief that bad things weren't supposed to happen to people like me. God simply asked me who I thought I was, and why I thought I was to be immune to the pains of this life. He spoke to my heart that I was exactly where He wanted me to be, because He was with me! He let me look around the Pediatric Intensive Care Unit at Children's Hospital in

> God simply asked me who I thought I was, and why I thought I was to be immune to the pains of this life.

Kansas City, and observe the hopelessness that so many experienced. He asked me who was best prepared to face this crisis? It was a humbling lesson, but one I needed. Then, eight months later, I faced the reality of Josh's heart surgery.

Following the second morning service that Sunday, this kind woman, who had been visiting our worship service for some time came up to me. She told me that she had a word from God for me. The word was that, if I had enough faith, Josh would not need this surgery, but it was dependent on my faith. I took her hand and asked her if she had enough faith for my son's healing, and she said yes. I looked her in the face and told her that on the basis of her faith my son would be healed. Josh had his six-hour heart reconstruction the next day as scheduled, and I never saw the lady again. She had no clue as to what she didn't know. What she called faith was stupidity, with good intent gone bad. She had no room in her belief system for God to be at work in this. I am not saying that God gave Josh his bad heart (again, I am not a fatalist), but I do believe He allowed it.

Some of my old Baptist friends were quite sure that Josh's heart was simply a consequence of my former life. That God was punishing me to the fourth generation. They drilled me to see if I really had confessed my sins. They assured me that this was a just punishment of God for my sin, a judgment. This was to make me feel better? In their belief system, there had to be a cause and effect. There are times that this is unquestionably true, but not always. Josh's heart couldn't just be the result of living in a fallen world. They had no room for the idea that bad things could happen to those seeking to live Godly lives. Something had to be wrong with me, or perhaps it was because my wife suffered from horrible allergies while carrying Josh. Maybe God was judging Dee (my wife) for marrying me, or because she used nose spray? There had to be some rational, logical, neat and tidy answer.

Some of my more fatalistic friends simply said it was God's will, and that God Himself had done this thing. They ascribe everything, like ancient Jews, to the hand of God. After all look at Job. OK, so I looked at Job, and saw that God allowed, not caused or orchestrated it. To my fatalist friends all things, good or bad, come from God. They sound like Muslims, with a Jesus flair! I believe that there is a huge difference in God allowing and God causing, God knowing and God predestining. The differences are gigantic!

So here I was, surrounded by all of my own friends, just like Job, and their idea of the counsel of God being spoken all around me. Here is what I learned: Josh's life caused me to trust Jesus more and to desperately depend on His grace. It revealed my inadequacy and my neediness. I know God allowed Josh to have a bad heart, but in no way did God strike him and predestine him to a heart condition. Josh's heart wasn't because of my past or my wife's allergies, but because we live on a fallen planet, where the pain of sin touches us all, even an innocent newborn. But in the middle of this life crisis the voice and presence of God was evident. He was with us every step of the way. His love was indescribably real and intimate. His encouragement was faithful. He fulfilled every promise in His Word to the letter. He gave peace in the middle of our storm, and we could see Him at work despite the tragic circumstance. Through this experience we learned so much about ourselves and our great and faithful Jesus!

> I believe that there is a huge difference in God allowing and God causing, God knowing and God predestining. The differences are gigantic!

Twenty-seven years later Josh serves as a full-time youth pastor with a most special view of life and service. He fully understands that his life is in the hands of his God. His life is a precious gift. Some of my Charismatic friends would benefit if they could learn to trust the same thing. They need to see that it takes more faith to walk in the valley than to be delivered out of it. My fatalistic friends with their clean theological system need to make room for life and the consequence of a fallen humanity that affects us with God's permission, not because He caused it. And for my Baptist friends, there need not always be a clear cut cause and effect. Every bad experience isn't the result of something we have done. Sometimes it is just the result of living. I can tell you that Josh's heart problem has worked for good. God has been faithful and His love lessons have been unbelievable!

The hardest thing for many in regard to trials or life crisis is whether they will be held responsible. Will they own up to what it is? It is fair to ask, is this a sin issue? For many it is a life issue. Will trust and love for God be enough, even when my world is turned upside down? Will I accept that bad things can come into my life and they can be for good, even though everything around me shouts bad. Can I accept things without a formula or having to see demons behind it?

A 16 year-old girl, who loves Jesus with all her heart, is killed by a drunk driver. Is this God's will? This is God's will only for theological fatalists and their very weird view of a loving God. Is it the work of the devil? After all, only he could do this. This works for the Charismatic but doesn't address the issue biblically or honestly. Is there a difference in saying that God allowed it but did not cause it? Can anything good come out of this? Mothers Against Drunk Drivers (MADD) was formed after an experience very similar to this. This doesn't remove the heartache or loss, but it shows how out of tragic circumstances good can come. It shows that God can do, in the midst of our crisis, what is His will, while the crisis itself is not His will, but the result of living in a fallen world.

> Will trust and love for God be enough, even when my world is turned upside down?

Some may have a problem with a crisis that appears to be "chance." Well, if you don't have room for it, you will have to develop systems that explain it away. You will develop arguments for God's existence that are circular, but convincing to the exclusion of anything that doesn't make sense. Brothers and sisters, sin doesn't make sense. God's forgiveness doesn't make sense, but we are grateful for it. I am not arguing for chance, but that there is a consequence of living in a fallen and sinful world that none of us can escape. The question remains how will you face the challenges of life crisis that will come your way?

How will you handle the crisis of a rebellious child who is living in self-destruct mode? How will you deal with financial failure that you had nothing to do with except that it affects your future? How will you deal with a spouse being diagnosed with a bi-polar condition? What if your wife is afflicted with MS or a disease that wasn't on your calendar? What if the church you have given your prime time to has decided that you are no longer a fit? What would you do if your spouse decided she no longer wanted to be married to you? What if your child declares he is "gay" or is moving in with his lover, can you cope? Does your faith allow such realities? What if your best friends in Christ, people you introduced to Christ and to each other, are murdered? I submit to you that some of these very storms will come your way. They never come with an invitation or when one might expect them. They are never welcomed guests, but always intruders. The way you respond reveals the truth about your walk with your God.

When Job heard his children had been killed, he prayed. What would you do? Would you show God your resume and argue that He has made a mistake!?! Would you say it is the will of Yahweh? How you answer will say volumes about your ability to truly minister to the people under your charge. It will reveal the heart that beats within your chest.

I spent years as a volunteer involved with an organization called Fellowship of Christian Athletes. It has always been ironic to me, since I am not an athlete, but my involvement was always a blast! I have often heard that sports build character. However, this isn't true. What is true is that playing the game can reveal character. When it is fourth down on your one yard line and the other team has the ball for the game's last play. If they score, they win, if not, you win. These moments reveal our character. What are you made of? What is your substance? The same can be said of our life's fourth-and-ones. They reveal our character, which in turn reveals our faith. Losing and winning both reveal aspects of our character and faith. What will a crisis greater than your ability to fix say about your faith? If you lose, what does your faith say? If bad things come your way, and they will, can you still trust in Christ? What if your story doesn't end as you had hoped? What if there is a death of someone you love, a spouse or a child? Can you still believe that all things work together for good?

When the storms come, when a crisis arises, I offer the following suggestions. First, don't let your circumstance diminish the truth of God's

Word. Do not surrender to feelings and emotions that all too often aren't true and for sure will not lead to peace. Second, do not allow the present crisis to erase the history of God's faithfulness both to you and to others. Third, don't look for a reason or answer more diligently than you cleave to His grace and the sufficiency of His love. Don't let your system of belief color a picture of God that may accommodate, but doesn't have the foundation of God's love to stand on. Fourth, know who your friends are, and remember there is One who is closer than a friend. Fifth, don't let the trauma of your situation cause you to despair or deny the only One who can truly heal and restore. Lastly, if you can look back at the faithful love of God in your past do not let the heartache of the present erode your hope in your future. In time, God can work even this crisis for good! In time, His love will again cover and heal. In time, His grace will prove to be sufficient. His time is always present and current, always on time, and always more than adequate for every crisis we will experience.

Life crisis is assured. Tragedy will one day knock at the door of your life. How you face it and respond to it will reveal the quality of your faith and say volumes about your character. Our character must speak of our faith. Men in times of war have shown great character and many times without any understanding of God. We, however, must reveal a character that points to faith. Our faith must speak to our hope and peace that is found only in the Lord Jesus.

So, when crisis or trials come into your life, welcome them as friends, so that your faith may produce a Godly steadfastness that gives birth to a deeper maturity. I don't think it is required to like the storm, but it is required to be like Christ in the middle of it. The storms are not for the faint of heart, but your endurance will serve to strengthen your heart. That a crisis will come is certain; how we respond is uncertain. One thing is certain, God's Word will not change, and I pray this will be the bedrock on which you are building your life in Christ.

For the Love of Money {16}

Do not lay up for yourselves treasures on earth, where moth and rust consume and where thieves break in and steal, but lay up for yourselves treasures in heaven, where neither moth nor rust consumes and where thieves do not break in and steal. For where your treasure is, there will your heart be also.   Matthew 6:19-21

One man gives freely, yet grows all the richer; another withholds what he should give, and only suffers want. A liberal man will be enriched and one who waters will himself be watered.   Proverbs 11:24-25

For the love of money is a root of all kinds of evil. Some people, eager for money, have wandered from the faith and pierced themselves with many griefs.   1 Timothy 6:10 (NIV)

As for the rich in this world, charge them not to be haughty, nor to set their hopes on the uncertain riches but on God who richly furnishes us with everything to enjoy. They are to do good, to be rich in good deeds, liberal and generous, thus laying up for themselves a good foundation for the future, so that they may take hold of the life which is life indeed.
1 Timothy 6:17-19

There are few areas that cause so much trouble among the ranks of the called as does the issue of money. The problems with money are common to all. For some there is never enough. For others it is an issue of being generous with what God has given them. For all it is a battle of obedient stewardship and biblical contentment. Most maintain that money is actually a neutral force that only has power given to it. Some like Richard Foster in his book, *Money, Sex and Power*, see money as an active power that influences our decisions and lives usually for the bad. I wish I could say that most ministers I know are above this struggle, but I can't. What I have seen are ministers who have learned to milk the system, churches who feel it is their charge to keep their ministers humble and faith-dependent by grossly underpaying them, ministers who justify godless behavior because of their paycheck, and churches that place their ministry staff in a position of desperation and difficulty because they refuse to pay them what they should.

Some ministers, who are in love with this world, are buried in irresponsible debt that testifies to their unquenchable thirst for stuff. How many ministers take a new church and immediately have to buy a new car as well as the new home? All the while, we are testifying to the truthfulness of Scripture in a negative way. We are sadly not unlike those we are to lead and help. How can I help another, when I can't help myself?

> More men have failed at the point of money than any other, even more than moral failure.

When I am buried in debt, don't pay my taxes, live above my means and still have a desire for more stuff, what do I do? If only I had more money. How can I take another vacation, when I haven't paid my mortgage? How can I buy a new car when I only make minimal credit card payments? What does this thirst for money say about my faith, my convictions, my integrity, my calling? When our lives are dominated by our debt and thirst for a quality of life we think we deserve, how can we lead a church or serve it when we aren't even following the Good Shepherd? How can I live contentedly when I thirst for more money?

Please listen! If we are going to make a difference, if we're going to lead, if we're going to model Christ, we have to resolve this issue regarding the love of money. More men have failed at the point of money than any other, even more than moral failure. The sad thing is that many are still in positions of leadership both in our churches and denominations. They, however, no longer follow Christ but their appetite for more and the things money can buy. Their discontent is evident, and the thirst of their soul is apparent.

Probably the best place to start is at the point of the transformation of our thinking. If we aren't transformed by the renewing of our minds, we are being conformed to the image of this world. We won't view the world, success, or money any different than any other natural man. At our best we will be carnal, babes in Christ, thinking and acting like those who don't know Christ. The evidence of a transformed mind is that now the principles of God's Word determine what we do and think regarding money. God's Word will set in motion our practice regarding money and how we live with it. If we are transformed by the renewing of our minds, it is apparent our view about wealth ought to be different than those who are outside of Christ. Does God's Word speak about debt, savings, spending and giving? What does the Bible say about contentment, and what does this have to say about my attitude towards money? All of these topics are addressed in the Scriptures, and there are many excellent books written from a biblical perspective about each one of them. However, there is still much that remains to be said and then done.

> One of the beginning indicators of true transformation of our minds is our ability to be content.

Unless God has your heart and mind and unless you are willing to submit to the principles of God's Word, contentment will never be something you experience. Without God's truth to guide us we will always be vulnerable to the multitude of ideas regarding the need to gain wealth. We will always make financial decisions on the basis of selfish gain rather than kingdom expansion. We will be more concerned with our well being than we are with obedience to God's Word. One of the beginning indicators of true transformation of our minds is our ability to be content.

Paul in a Roman prison put it this way in Philippians 4:11-13 "Not that I complain of want; for I have learned, in whatever state I am, to be content. I know how to be abased, and I know how to abound; in any and all circumstances I have learned the secret of facing plenty and hunger, abundance and want. I can do all things in him who strengthens me." This is the testimony of a transformed mind. Will I allow God to shape my thinking? Will I allow His Word and not the world to determine my thinking? Will His Word or my appetite determine my financial outcomes?

Contentment in any situation is possible only as I am in Him and as I daily die to self (that ol' discipleship stuff!). Contentment is found in Him. By this I mean, and I think Paul meant, that only as God's will regarding this world, becomes my will, will I be able to see wealth for what it is. Am I wealthy because I have money in the bank and more on the way? Is my wealth defined by what I can buy or afford to buy based on my credit report? As a Christian my wealth ought to be defined by where I am, and that ought to be my position in Christ. The problem is that I am always vulnerable to the lust of the eyes and pride of life, the things that money can buy.

I counter this by fleshing out Galatians 2:20 (NIV) "I have been crucified with Christ; and I no longer live, but Christ lives in me. The life I live in the body, I live by faith in the Son of God, who loved me and gave himself for me." Only as I find my contentment in my relationship with Christ will I discover true contentment in living. It is only at the point of my submission to His will and word that His power breaks my thirst for money and the things it affords. I need money to live in this world, but I do not need to be under its yoke of slavery.

> I believe my spiritual contentment is first and foremost seen at the point of my tithing.

One place where contentment is revealed is at the point of my giving. If I withhold what I should give, I am only revealing my discontentment and disobedience. I am a person who believes I am to be a biblical Christian, not just a New Testament believer. By this I mean that much of the Old Testament is still applicable for me today. Jesus came to fulfill the old Law, not do away with it. That is why I believe my spiritual contentment is first and foremost seen at the point of my tithing. I believe that the tithe is the beginning point of my trusting God's Word, not the end point.

The tithe literally means a tenth, so that is where I believe my steward-ship begins. From the very beginning of our marital journey my wife and I began taking Malachi 3:6-10 literally—where I believe I am charged to bring the whole tithe to God. We have seen this as the beginning point, never the ending point. A person who is discontent can never give ten per-cent, because they can't see how they can make it without the money. After all they have debt to pay, and God doesn't need the money.

The second point of our stewardship is found in 2 Corinthians 9:6-15 where I am challenged to be a generous giver. The context is a special offer-ing being collected for the hurting saints back in Jerusalem. The offering was voluntary, but if one gave, it needed to be generous and in faith. It was also to be given with joy not because it had to be given. There is no contentment in giving under compulsion. For me the principle is that God wants me to be a generous giver, who gives above my tithe to special needs and circumstances. This is only possible if I am content and my life is not swallowed up in debt. Which leads to the next area of contentment—no or minimal debt.

As it is with contentment and giving, much has been written and taught about the evils of debt, but yet too many ministers remain incarcer-ated (literally!) by debt. This is plain and simply a testimony to discontent-ment—after all I deserve all the stuff debt acquires, right? Bankruptcies are epidemic in the United States, and Christians are well represented in the bankruptcy courts. In a nutshell, when I owe someone I am techni-cally their slave, and they are my master. If I owe more than I can pay, I am technically a thief. All this is brought to you by the love of money. We buy homes we cannot afford, and then we are suffocating in debt. We buy cars because we can make the monthly payment for the next 72 months, provided we never get sick, miss work, have an emergency, lose our jobs, or whatever. We have great credit because we have debt and make minimal payments. The problem is that debt becomes our master, and we become its slave. We are truly in prison to debt.

Think about what Jesus said in Matthew 6:24 (NIV) "No one can serve two masters. Either he will hate the one and love the other, or he will be devoted to the one and despise the other. You cannot serve both God and Money." There are many Christian views on debt that range from having no debt to having manageable debt. I am an advocate of the latter. By manageable, I mean that debt does not prohibit my ability to tithe or give above my tithe. Manageable means I live within my means, not based on my wants or desires. Manageable means that if I lost my income I could liquidate my "stuff" and be able to pay off all my debt and have monies left over. It means that I don't live on speculative guesses concerning income or values of property but actual values and actual incomes.

Where I live in Colorado, paying cash for a home would be virtually impossible for most people, but buying a home within one's reality, that does not impede giving is always possible. Plus, a wise home investment would allow one to sell the property (for profit) for much less than market values if the need ever occurred. It will mean buying a smaller or older home than the real estate sales person might say you can afford. The issue is whose voice will we listen to? God wants us to be content; the world wants us to get all we deserve and want, what we cannot afford. It also means being wise with our finances and being willing to stay in one place instead of constantly "trading up." The object is to get out of debt as quickly as possible. This will not happen if I am discontent and want more. It is all about the love of money. What is your objective: to please God or live in a kingdom of excessive debt?

> The issue is whose voice will we listen to? God wants us to be content; the world wants us to get all we deserve and want, what we cannot afford.

Land and property have historically been good investments, even with debt, but make sure they address an honest need and not just a material want. Make sure that your goal is contentment, not gain. Again the testimony is contentment, not how big one's house is. Your home will either possess you, or you will possess it. If your mind is being transformed, you will not be beguiled by the lust of the eye.

Another area to be cautious about is debt on cars. A rule of thumb is to never buy new. The minute you have driven off the lot your value drops a minimum of 20%. To purchase a car on a long term loan insures going into long term debt on a depreciable item that is not an investment but an expense. We need automobiles, but we don't need most of what we want. Keep your car well maintained, and you will be able to keep your car much longer than the average owner regardless of mileage. Purchase what is needed and affordable. For example, where I live almost everyone who moves here automatically thinks they need (ugh!) a four-wheel drive vehicle. The truth is you don't. In the last 19 years I can count on one hand the times I actually needed four-wheel drive to get around. When the weather is that bad, no one needs to be out anyway. Plus, four-wheel drives get atrocious gas mileage; they have many more mechanical issues than do a standard front-wheel drive. But they are so cool and everyone has one! Their annual cost is easily twice that of a front-wheel drive. For the love of money!

> If you aren't careful you will discover the Mr. Hyde side of credit card companies, when you can't make a payment.

The point is, be content. Drive what you need not what you want or think you deserve. Never ever drive a car someone has convinced you that you can afford. Lastly, a point of prejudice that is tragically true. Your wisest choice of vehicles will almost always be Japanese. Why? Because they build cars that are reliable and dependable. Sadly, the same isn't usually true of their American counterparts. To verify my prejudice, pick up a copy of *Consumer Reports*. OK, I know it isn't the Bible, and the Bible doesn't say too much about which car to drive, but it does speak a lot about wisdom and gaining counsel for wise choices.

Another area that says a lot about our heart's attitude regarding money is our use of credit cards. Many Christian counselors simply tell us to get rid of them. For many of us that is the best counsel. There is perhaps another option. Only use your credit card for amounts you have in the bank, and pay off your credit card every month. This takes discipline, but if you don't have the money in the bank, don't use a credit card!

Never buy something today that you will have to wait until next month to (hopefully) have the money to pay for. One of the evils of credit cards is the ease with which one can make purchases and how, without paying attention, can very rapidly find oneself in a debt trap. Regardless of what the commercials say, banks and credit companies aren't there to serve you; they are there to make a profit, even if it ensnares you. If you aren't careful you will discover the Mr. Hyde side of credit card companies, when you can't make a payment. Another danger with credit cards is the ease with which you can buy something you have absolutely no need of. If you didn't need it before you saw it, don't buy it. But credit cards make this so easy to do. The best policy for most is to use credit cards sparingly and only if you have the money in the bank to cover the charge. I know some who love to play with credit cards by constantly moving their accounts around getting lower interest and/or no interest transfers. These folks spend way to much time on the computer and have more energy than most of us do. Far too many folks like this are just one step ahead of creditors. The best plan for ones future is trusting God, the second is the elimination of debt.

Now, think about something I have already written about. If I am in a church situation and am discontented with what I make, I must answer a few questions. Why am I in this line of work? Worldly wealth is not the objective for most who follow this vocational path. There are some exceptions. I know some denominational workers and pastors who live well above the norm and will retire quite comfortably. I even know some missionaries who will retire with quite a lot of wealth to tide them over. I know we aren't to say anything bad about missionaries, but in all honesty some live quite well in their foreign setting and have become just another colonialist, and when they come home, they will live very nicely. Some of the perks given to denominational workers are only matched by that of CEOs and long-term union workers. I need not even mention the dishonest, unethical TV evangelists who live in million dollar homes, drive a Mercedes Benz, and all the while are begging you to give them your last dollar. These, I pray, are the exception.

Now back to the main issue. If I am discontent with my current salary, I must ask some questions. First, am I living within my means or has my desire and want exceeded my ability to pay? Second, was I deceived in what

I was led to believe I would be making? If so, the church has integrity issues, and another decision needs to be made. Third, even if my pay is poor, am I honestly earning my paycheck, or have I begun playing the comparison game? Laziness is a horrible sin among the ranks of the ordained, especially among those who feel they are underpaid. When I develop an attitude that I am worth more than I am being paid, I need to find another line of work.

The exception is when I am working my hardest, giving more than what is expected, and I can't live on what I make. Don't be afraid to go to the leadership of the church in a proper way and time. Go to them after much prayer to share your situation. Approach the church's leadership honestly and respectfully. If they are unwilling to seek possible solutions, another decision regarding your tenure might have to be made. If the church honestly can't give me enough to live on, I must prayerfully decide if it's time to move on or trust God for His provision outside of the church. Be cautious of comparisons; they are usually wrong and ultimately very destructive to ones performance and attitude. Remember why we work— for the glory of God, and we do all things in His name. Yes, I know we have family needs and other concerns, but I believe our biggest concern ought to be the integrity of our work, not the size of our paycheck.

> Remember that we don't do our vocation for the love of money, but the love of Jesus, and ultimately it is in Him we trust.

Lastly, if I am working with Holy integrity, honestly doing above what is required, and I can't live on the salary given, I must make a decision. If it results in my leaving, I must leave graciously. Many churches want to do more but are unable to do so, it is just reality. Remember that we don't do our vocation for the love of money, but the love of Jesus, and ultimately it is in Him we trust. Remember that the church can only give what it has.

I have also seen pastors who chose to have huge families and then dumped guilt on the church to accommodate their choice. This is bogus and irresponsible. If I have one child or twelve, that is my choice and not the church's burden to bear unless they, without compulsion, chose to take up the responsibility. If you want to have a gigantic family, God bless you! But don't dump the responsibility for your choice on the very people you say you are called to serve. All too often the church suffers because so much time is given to caring for the family. Be very careful at this point, because it reveals one's integrity.

If you are a pastor, remember you are responsible for taking care of your staff. The church depends on you to give honest assessments of the needs of staff and the need for staff. The staff is not to make the pastor look good, but this is often the understood reality. The pastor is to ensure that the ministry team is taken care of and adequately provided for, even if it means he doesn't get a raise when they do. I have seen churches give their pastor huge raises, while giving their staff only cost of living increases. This is many times unethical! I know pastors who constantly bemoan the shortage of staff in their churches, while it never occurred to them that their pay is so high the church can't afford more. They can't have it both ways.

Finally, honor God with your wealth. Be a generous giver, one who understands both the obligation and the privilege. Don't give God minimums, but all. In all honesty He already owns it; we are simply stewards. The question is what type of steward will we prove to be? Live within your means and be content. Rejoice with those who have more and mourn for those with less, but be content in any and every situation. In the eyes of the world, every American is filthy rich, and we really are. Check your attitude. Keep a close eye on your work ethic; never be called lazy. Never allow your boss, church or leaders to think that you aren't giving your all. Don't play the comparisons game. This is just a gimmick of the devil and exposes underlying discontentment. Keep debt in check and live within your means. Be wary of credit cards and the insatiable thirst for "new." Remember that your treasure reveals the location of your heart. So, in conclusion, what is it going to be, the love of money or the love of God? The decision is yours.

The Church: The Body of Christ

And they devoted themselves to the apostles' teaching and fellowship, to the breaking of bread and the prayers. **Acts 2:42**

Christ is the head of the church, his body, of which he is the Savior. **Ephesians 5:23b (NIV)**

And His gifts were that some should be apostles, some prophets, some evangelists, some pastors and teachers, to equip the saints for the work of ministry, for building up the body of Christ, until we all attain to the unity of the faith and of the knowledge of the Son of God, to mature manhood, to the measure of the stature of the fullness of Christ; so that we may no longer be children, tossed to and fro and carried about by every wind of doctrine. **Ephesians 4:11-14a**

From mega-churches to home churches, most everyone in ministry desires to be a part of a legitimate, authentically relevant New Testament church. I have known numerous church planters, who assertively announced they were starting a New Testament church, as if every other church that has been started in the last 50 years is less than New Testament. But this really does beg a question. What does a New Testament church look like? Some churches are in hot pursuit of signs and wonders with a special dash of the Holy Spirit anointing. Some churches run like IBM and are every bit as efficient with the blue suits to boot! (I know IBM no longer requires blue suits, but these churches do!)

Some claim there is a movement of God in the area of house churches, though honest documentation is seriously lacking or insufficient to call it a movement just yet (I am aware of only one source that is regularly quoted to substantiate a house church movement). Some churches are casual; some are very formal; some churches are liturgical in nature, while others are off the charts and off the walls! So, what exactly is a New Testament church? What are the necessary ingredients that make a church New Testament? How does the church act like a body, if it is modeled after a corporation?

Another question is, what is the New Testament model for church leadership and polity? Like the first question there are numerous answers and all are given with equal conviction. Southern Baptists argue for congregational rule, even making it part of their *Baptist Faith and Message*. The *BF&M* is a non-binding, binding doctrinal creedal statement that is not called a creedal statement, though it really is a creedal statement. It should be noted that most of the mega- SBC churches and many of the medium sized are really led by the pastoral staff rather than the congregation.

> Seminaries exist to train professionally "called" ministers to do the ministry that the Bible says the individual saints are to be doing.

Methodists have their own system; Assemblies of God have a system like the Methodists; Charismatics are pastor-centered and, because he is anointed of God, he is almost virtually untouchable, unless something in the closet springs up and exposes him, and even then it may not be fatal. The Bible Churches and Presbyterians have elders, which at least has a biblical precedent. Not to suggest that the others don't, but theirs is more of a stretch biblically speaking. This can go on and on, so I'll get to the point.

The beginning point of the church begins with what we know from Scripture. We know that the Scripture calls the church the body of Christ. Pastors, teachers, evangelists and the like are to equip the saints (individual members of the body) to do the ministry of building up the body of Christ (Ephesians 4:11-12). Seminaries exist to train professionally "called" ministers to do the ministry that the Bible says the individual saints are to be doing. So one thing is very obvious—if there is precedent for how ministry to the body is to take place, we then have already altered the formula. What did the early disciples do? It is clear that they were teachers of the words of Christ. They had just spent three years of their lives with Him! They were the living record of His teaching. The saints, the individual parts of the body, joined the Apostles for this teaching, fellowship and prayer. We know that at least some of the Apostles modeled evangelistic preaching, such as Peter at Pentecost and following days. It is no wonder that Stephen and Phillip were so motivated to do evangelism. They had seen the apostle do it. So, at its core, the church was to be a place of teaching, prayer and fellowship. This is still a very real quality in many different style churches in the world today. Could it be that the Scripture is less concerned with form than it is with the church's function?

The first deacons were elected to care for the needs of people within the church so as not to interfere with the Apostles' teaching and praying. But those wild and crazy deacons started preaching, and soon they caused a riot against the church. If only they had stuck to the waiting on tables thing! But they did imitate what they saw the apostles do, didn't they?

Many of the signs of the Spirit found in Acts are clearly to show that the church and subsequently the Kingdom of God, was now expanding beyond the Jewish community. Some would try to standardize tongues, healings and such as critical parts of the core church teaching. It is probably best left for the theologians to argue, but it is undeniable that, as the church grew and matured, there was diminishing evidence of signs and wonders. There is very little similarity in what are today called signs and wonders. It must be understood that miracles in the book of Acts were never advertised and announced to take place on a given Sunday, ("Come to Healing Service this Sunday featuring the Apostle Paul, with his healing hands of fire!") but happened as the Kingdom of God was penetrating the darkness of the lost world. The Son of God had risen; He was Lord over all, even Caesar! I really think that many false teachers would be silenced if they were forced to really do what they say they are anointed to do. For example, most of Paul's miraculous events took place in the market place of life, were the masses of people were found, as was true with Jesus. Every preacher who claims to be a healer should be required to visit hospitals in every town he visits to do his thing, or be silenced as a fake!

Every healing in Scripture had a purpose and revealed something about the majesty of God and Jesus His Son. The miracles verified the power of the resurrection and the expansion of God's Kingdom on the earth. Today it has become a cheap sideshow that probably was born out of true but misguided intention. Suffice it to say that for me, as I understand the Word of God, signs and wonders have had their place, but not as core teaching in the church. Back to the task at hand!

At the center of the Church are teaching, praying and fellowship. We also see the evidence in Acts of the power the early church's witness, which is a primary reason the Holy Spirit came. But what does the Scripture say about form of church government? As I understand Scripture, the only model mentioned is that of a plurality of elders in each city. This is primarily the method employed by Paul. Why elders?

Hebrews 13:7 says, "Remember your leaders (elders), those who spoke to you the word of God; consider the outcome of their life, and imitate their faith." The writer goes on to say in Hebrews 13:17, "Obey your leaders and submit to them; for they are keeping watch over your souls, as men who will have to give account. Let them do this joyfully, and not sadly, for that would be of no advantage to you." Paul put it this way in Titus 1:5, "This is why I left you in Crete, that you might amend what was defective, and appoint elders in every town as I directed you." Paul then goes on and gives a clear description of what an elder looked like, as he did in his first letter to Timothy. It is appropriate to perhaps use the idea of pastor as well as elder, but the word is elder, overseer, not pastor, though the function has evolved into virtually the same thing. The evolution of the function is without question, but the term was and still is elder.

> It is tragic when pastors today don't measure up to the standard of elder. It is inexcusable!

The Scriptures don't talk about how often the elders met or their age (though older is clearly meant) or how long they served—all of which allows for a lot of latitude. The quality of their lives and integrity of their faith, however, is clearly defined and specific.

I think it is clear why Paul established elders. As older men both physically and spiritually, they would insure the purity and quality of the teaching within the new churches. These elders were almost always deeply connected to Paul or one of his key men. In the Baptist tradition deacons have many times been given elder function without meeting the biblical qualification. The results have often been regrettable. It is even more tragic when pastors today don't measure up to the standard of elder. It is inexcusable!

So the leader, elder, pastor was to lead out in teaching, praying and fellowship (not eating fried chicken!) and witness. Paul put it this way in Philippians 4:9 (NIV) "Whatever you have learned or received or heard from me, or seen in me—put it into practice. And the God of peace will be with you." This is what an elder, a leader, a pastor-teacher is to be doing. So regardless of the 'shape' of the congregation you are aligned with, the functionary role is to equip the saints by both what we say and do.

It probably goes without saying that God is more concerned with the quality of life of those leading than He is if they have business meetings monthly or quarterly. God probably doesn't care if you meet in a home, cathedral, or garage, as long as the Word is correctly taught, prayer is practiced, true fellowship occurs and there is power in your witness. It is doubtful that there is a movement of God afloat exclusively with any particular church model, but God will breathe life into any model that is submitted to Christ as its head.

> The only church that isn't persecuted is the western church. In our affluence we argue over preaching styles, forms of worship and polity, a luxury the rest of the world doesn't enjoy.

In the days the Scriptures were written, the church met in homes, along rivers, underground, wherever they could gather safely. They were facing issues we can't even imagine. But much of the church in the world today can! The only church that isn't persecuted is the western church.

In our affluence we argue over preaching styles, forms of worship and polity, a luxury the rest of the world doesn't enjoy. I just returned from the Muslim area of West Africa. In one remote village the little church structure had been torn down four times and the pastor (a bi-vocational farmer) had been arrested. He can't read or write, but I think he does the basics of church better than most of his USA counterparts. In his village we met under a tree, as we did in many of the villages we visited.

Another key for the church in the early days was flexibility and fluidness. We have forgotten something in the West. We are often more concerned with our methods than we are many times with biblical principles. The persecuted church stands on biblical principles and doesn't have time to worry about methodology.

As I observe the American church, I see the mega-church where seekers can come and just be invisible and never belong. Is this what church was meant to be? I see church "lite," accepting everyone and everything. They are without discernment and pass no judgment, therefore they have a lower moral and ethical bar of behavioral expectation. Their message is always "uplifting" and "relevant"(!?).

> I dare say that if our circumstances were different, if we faced what the first century faced, much of what we accept would not be accepted.

There are churches where you can just attend, and never have to join, since (they say) membership isn't biblical anyway. So, "we aren't asking if you aren't telling," is the mantra, because they don't know!

Then we ask the question, who is the church? Who are our services for anyhow? Does doctrine even matter? We have big-name Charismatic evangelists who don't even believe in the Trinity and others who are nothing more than Christianized therapists preaching a cross-less, sinless, and bloodless message of "God accepts you just the way you are!" I dare say that if our circumstances were different, if we faced what the first century faced, much of what we accept would not be accepted. We need to, regardless of our form, get back to the basics of what church is to be, the body of Christ!

So what do I conclude? My opinions may not be adequate for some, but they work well for me. 1) Do the Word, prayer, fellowship and witness well. 2) My primary task as pastor is to equip, truly equip, the body to do the work of ministry for the building up of the body of Christ. 3) I am to model what I teach. That means it is critical for me to walk my talk. 4) And the last thing I would mention is that I am to be a servant.

Because we think we can make anyone a leader, our emphasis tends to be on style and technique. We really aren't raising up leaders, but managers (as previously noted) who think they are! We aren't raising up servants but men who are above doing the menial. Our ultimate example of leadership is Christ. He said he came to serve, not be served. We haven't got it yet! The last significant thing He did with his disciples before His arrest was to wash their feet. He told them if them if they did as He had done to them, they would be blessed. I can only assume that too many of us aren't very blessed. Consider John 13:12-17,

> When he had washed their feet, and taken his garments, and resumed his place, he said to them, "Do you know what I have done to you? You call me Teacher and Lord; and you are right, for so I am. If I then your Lord and teacher, have washed your feet, you also ought to wash one another's feet. For I have given you an example, that you also should do as I have done to you. Truly, truly, I say to you , a servant, is not greater than his master; nor is he who is sent greater than he who sent him. If you know these things, blessed are you if you do them'"

I would like to share three personal experiences that relate in very different ways to servitude. Two experiences took place while I was in seminary, and one while I was serving as a pastor. While in seminary I worked on campus as a janitor, or as I called it a "John Boy." One day I was cleaning a bathroom on the campus (as I related earlier) thinking that here I was with a college degree cleaning toilets! I remember thinking, Story, you are really going places! About this time God spoke to me, about me. He gently told me that until I learned the "lesson of the porcelain" I had nothing to say to anybody! I didn't like the lesson, but I never forgot it. What I gained from this was that there is no task I am too good for, and I am above nothing. I mention this story again because I also gained the idea that I would never ask another to do something I was unwilling to do myself. I have tried to live by a standard that I ask guys to do what I am doing, and not what I don't do. It is like sermons. I want to make sure that to the best of my ability I am trying to flesh out what I am preaching about.

The second experience occurred later that same year. I was carrying a bag full of dirty mop heads to the maintenance building. I saw a guy in a white Cadillac Eldorado. He waved me over to his car. He was obviously a preacher, judging by his dress and hairstyle. He was in town for our denomination's convention. He asked me if I knew where a golf course was. I didn't but told him I'd find out where one was located. So I asked some other students where one was, and gave the man the information. Then, to my surprise, He said to me, "You look like an intelligent young man, so I want to give you something you will appreciate." I thought it was going to be some money, which would have been nice, since I was poor! Instead he handed me his autographed business card, and then without missing a beat gave me a self-autographed copy of a graduation sermon he had been preaching for the last 25 years (this is not an exaggeration!). He told me that because I was obviously so bright he wanted me to have both of these valued gifts. All I could say was, "Oh WOW! Thank You So Much," in my best Steve Martin impersonation! This guy really thought himself to be something special, helping a poor seminary student with autographed copies of his ego! I don't think this is what Jesus had in mind. I have a hard time carrying business cards to this day!

> Why do you think Jesus' last act was to wash the disciples' feet? How are you doing following His example?

The third story took place while I was involved in a training conference on some new discipleship materials. We were at a denominational retreat center. It was just an intimate group of those who would be leading the sessions. The author of the materials led us in a foot washing service. It was an humbling and encouraging time for everyone involved. The next day, however, the leader informed us that he had been reprimanded and told by his superiors that we don't wash feet. I wish I could say this was just an isolated incident. But all too often there is never a servant in the house. Pastors run around like God's little dumplings and are just too busy; denominational workers are just above it, and too many of our missionaries are too busy being strategists to wash any one's feet. We teach how to be the boss but don't have a clue how to serve. We teach how to be and look professional but never offer an opportunity to wash someone's feet. We have made pride a virtue and disdain any acts of humility and service.

Why do you think Jesus' last act was to wash the disciples' feet? How are you doing following His example? This is the fourth and final key ingredient in what I believe is to be essential for the church to be genuine. Servitude is incredibly important and usually neglected. I believe servitude is part of the glue that holds the body together. It is the key to our leadership. We aren't worthy of leadership until we learn the lessons of humility. Humility is at the heart of the body of Christ!

The Differences Between Dreamers, Visionaries, and the Strategies of Men {18}

> So I came to Jerusalem and was there three days. Then I arose in the
> night, I and a few men with; and I told no one what my God had put
> into my heart to do for Jerusalem.   Nehemiah 2:11-12

> So the wall was finished on the twenty-fifth day of the month Elul, in
> fifty-two days. And when all our enemies heard of it, all the nations
> round about us were afraid and fell greatly in their own esteem; for
> they perceived that this work had been accomplished with the help of
> our God.   Nehemiah 6:15-16

> And now, behold, the cry of the people of Israel has come to me, and I
> have seen the oppression with which the Egyptians oppress them. Come,
> I will send you to Pharaoh that you may bring forth my people, the sons
> of Israel, out of Egypt. But Moses said to God, "Who am I that I should
> go to Pharaoh, and bring the sons of Israel out of Egypt?" He said, "But
> I will be with you; and this shall be the sign for you, that I have sent;
> when you have brought forth the people out of Egypt, you shall serve
> God upon this mountain."   Exodus 2:9-12

I recently attended a conference where one of the keynote speakers said, "If we are to start a movement of God, we must…" Does anything sound wrong with this line of thinking? Has the human mind grown so powerful, so spiritual, that now out of our own abilities we can start a movement of God? I hear things like, "total gospel saturation!" Or we must take the gospel to the world so Jesus can come back. So we target on people groups of over 250,000 to reach with gospel saturation. The problem is that we didn't even saturate the smaller subgroups. I believe we have no concept of what that really means, except it sounds so godly! As my mentor Max Barnett has asked, "What is our strategy or vision for reaching Iran?" There really is no vision, but there are plenty of big strategies and even bigger dreams.

I am not trying to be unjustly critical of godly people having dreams, but I do think we need to have some concept of what we really are saying. What is the difference between dreams and vision? The following definitions are mine, and you should develop your own.

Dreams: Ideas that are enormous in scope and nonspecific in objective. They seemingly are God-sized and God-dependent, but because of their vagueness, they are impossible to measure. It may center around one denominational group or a specific person. It would take God to accomplish it and usually has a sense of biblical mooring, but because of the generalized nature there often is no specific plan (most of the plans are just rewrapped ideas that a particular group prefers) to attempt accomplishment in legitimate ways. Dreams usually die with one professing them and usually become the impetus for another program.

> Dreams are seemingly God-sized and God-dependent, but because of their vagueness, they are impossible to measure.

For example, it is without question that we are to be involved in the fulfillment of the Great Commission. Our insanity is that we have done a poor, though earnest, job in the non-10/40 areas of the world (the ones outside the equatorial regions), so now we are going to take that same sincere ineptness to the unreached people in the 10/40 window. Great! How? How can people who have not been evangelizing in their known world be empowered to do it in a hard soil that is still so hostile to the gospel? This line of thinking doesn't even have biblical support! The USA is rapidly becoming a country with little or no Christian influence. Perhaps it is because we thought God was a Republican or that a peanut farmer from Georgia was *His* man! We struggle with our own logjam, so we must be more careful in removing the splinter from another country's eye.

I am not even suggesting that we stop trying; we should try harder! But we need to be careful what we call it. I remember that my own denomination boldly claimed that we would have taken the gospel to the known world before now, and we haven't. It isn't for lack of trying or desire, or even prayer. The fact is that the number of non-Christians is growing exponentially. Our error is not from a lack of effort, but in not realizing that vision does not come from a committee, or a think tank or even some spiritual gurus who see themselves as visionaries. Dreams do, but not vision! No denomination will achieve this, ever! Even when we work with other like-hearted groups, it needs to be understood that it cannot be done with human ingenuity, but it will demand human effort. All of us working together, rather than in sectarian camps, will be required to make inroads but even doing this insures nothing!

There is nothing wrong with having dreams. They are a good thing, but they become dangerous when they are what drive us. We can claim anything from 'movements of God' to 'world gospel saturation' as long as we deal with non-specifics and never truly develop litmus tests for success. It can keep denominational programmers employed, if they never have to give an account of their failures. Pastors are just as guilty on the local level.

Vision: A God sized challenge that is dependent on God to accomplish. Vision requires measurable faith and obedience. Vision is specific. The origin is God and probably won't become a best seller! The specific nature allows God to use His

> God-given vision will always outlive the one by whom it came. Visions are never about the one through whom they are given.

called ones to determine under His Spirit's leadership the strategies for accomplishment. The strategies are huge but God centered/dependent, and measurable. They always center on bringing glory to God. They might be focused on things of a redemptive nature or they might focus on His church. God-given visions are always consistent with God's Word, will, purpose and provision. God-given vision will always outlive the one by whom it came. Visions are never about the one through whom they are given. biblical vision requires and depends on *God* to be accomplished rather than the efforts of man (I am not suggesting any form of fatalism). It is possible for the very ones whom God wants to work with to miss the vision of God—check out Israel in the wilderness. Vision can be quenched.

God spoke to Nehemiah's heart and called him to rebuild the wall of Jerusalem. With God's plan, Nehemiah's obedience, the people's effort and courage and God's power, it was accomplished. The enemies of God were afraid because they said it could not be done. They were right, but also horribly wrong, because they did not know or understand God and how when He gives vision He will give all that is required to finish it.

God spoke to Moses and called him to rescue His people. God empowered him, prepared him and sent him. God allowed Moses to fill in the blanks, but there was no mistaking it was God's plan—God's vision for His people. God's vision demanded faith and obedience out of Moses and required God's power to be accomplished. The people demonstrated that they could grieve God's will and therefore miss the very thing God's vision had for them. Numbers chapter 13 is a tragic record of faithlessness, except for Joshua and Caleb. But the next generation experienced the purpose of God that was born out of His vision for *His* people (as did Joshua and Caleb). The children of Israel have never gotten over God delivering them from the slavery of Egypt thousands of years later.

Again there is nothing wrong with having grand dreams for the glory of God, as long as we recognize it may not be a vision given by God for God's people or glory. We preacher types have a hard enough time knowing the difference between our opinion and God's principles, let alone God's vision from my dreams.

Other men of vision would be men like Hudson Taylor, Dawson Trotman, Bill Bright, and others. I know few men of vision who happen to be pastors. I have known some who were church planters; some appear to be true visionaries but time will tell. I think there is a great pastor in California for whom time will someday attest his vision. I think I know some missionaries who truly are visionary, but they are the exception rather than rule.

A common trait among people of vision is their humility. Another is an overwhelming sense of inadequacy! These are not common characteristics found in our churches, leadership or missionary forces. These individuals are willing to experience great personal sacrifice for what they believe to be the vision God has given them. They are virtually consumed by the vision, and it does consume them! Remember God-given vision incorporates God's people, their need, their plight, their call, and the glory of God. They are very biblical, for it is within the context of the Bible that their vision has its parameters and context. Most of the time the visionary will not be the most popular or in step with the latest church growth trends. They aren't a good fit for a lot of things that men strategize about. They may not be deemed good team players. But they are men of vision, God-given vision.

Someone may be thinking that this is splitting hairs, but it isn't. We are surrounded by those who purport to be motivated by what they call a vision. But is it really? Is it for the Kingdom of God; is it for the people of God; is it for the glory of God? Does it depend on Jesus to succeed? Is it measurable and clear in its objective? Does it require sacrifice and biblical faith rooted in obedience? Is it clear in its purpose? If you

> Visionaries are willing to experience great personal sacrifice for what they believe to be the vision God has given them.

can answer yes to these questions, you are probably involved in the fleshing out of a vision. If no, it is probably not much more than a pipe dream or another man-initiated program!

To be sure, some can have all of the above regarding our particular ministries or churches and fall within the parameters of vision. This is true and accurate. It is also a part of vision—by that I mean that the church's expansion is part of God's plan for Kingdom expansion as found in Scripture. I can be one part of this great purpose and be active in God's visional purpose and still not be a visionary. If I see hundreds of churches, and as a result structure and sacrifice and plan and pray for God to be glorified through what I know is His will, I might be visionary. If I say I see thousands of churches being started out of my congregation of 25, and go around claiming land and people for the kingdom, I may be nothing more than a dreamer. If I profess a promise from God and never take the time to develop a workable measurable strategy that legitimately requires God to intervene, I am just a dreamer. Dreamers are good, but sometimes unfruitful and often ineffective. Visionaries are consumed with passion and driven to achieve the vision they are consumed by. Visionaries don't tend to get caught up in detours or side issues. Consider Nehemiah 6:3b "I am doing a great work and I cannot come down. Why should the work stop while I leave it and come down to you?"

Strategists: Those God uses to map out the steps which, through prayer and sacrifice, it is believed will lead to the fulfillment of God's vision. Or simply, persons who put together man-conceived plans and programs based more on theory than prayerful obedience. Words, like planning, demographics, economics, and geographic influences are their verbiage. They may be theorists or builders, architects of God's plan or proprietors of man conceived programs. Time and activity exposes them for what they are.

I have observed that in missions and denominational life we sometimes (*not always!*) move an ineffective field missionary or staff member into a position that is called 'strategist.' Tragically, this type of strategist may be the largest representative of the title. We are so afraid of admitting a guy is not getting it done, or that he is incompetent or that he is basically failing in a position, we cover it over by moving him to another position, all too often calling him a strategist.

> Strategists are persons who put together man-conceived plans and programs based more on theory than prayerful obedience.

I have aspirations to own property on the French Mediterranean and a châteaux in the Swiss Alps. I can see myself driving the Lotus and a Ferrari that I keep in my Rocky Mountain getaway. Do I need to go on?

This is exactly what some people would call vision, but it is nothing more than a pipe dream. A vision is big but measurable, dependent on God and requires my involvement. A vision is consistent with God's purpose, not my success, because it is about His reputation not mine

Vision brings clarity and direction; dreams are colorful and big but suffer from lack of clarity of direction and implementation. Vision allows objective measuring to determine progress, dreams have huge numbers and ideas that are beyond reason. Dreams sound so rooted in faith, when in reality they are foolish, because they will never be realized, but they sound so noble! For example, we know God loves the world. We say we will take the gospel to every human being by the year 2025 (in this example). How are we going to do that in all of Iran, Iraq, Afghanistan, Turkey, etc.? I know we have dedicated people in all of those places and send short term "prayer walking mission teams" to those areas, but it still does not address how we will see this done. How do we pray intelligently for this type of thinking? In my state we say we want everyone to hear the gospel. How? How do we begin to reach every tourist and person on vacation? How will we do this, how will we know when we have done it? Is this driven by bad eschatology or just a good-intentioned dream gone bad? Regardless, it isn't a God-given vision.

Are the Fields Really White for Harvest?

> Do you not say, "There are yet four months, then comes the harvest?"
> I tell you, lift up your eyes, and see how the fields are already white
> for harvest.   John 4:35

> A sower went out to sow. And as he sowed, some seeds fell along the
> path, and the birds came and devoured them. Other seeds fell on rocky
> ground, where they had not much soil, and immediately they sprang
> up, since they had no depth of soil, but when the sun rose they were
> scorched and since they had no root they withered away. Other seeds
> fell upon thorns, and the thorns grew up and choked them. Other seeds
> fell on good soil and brought forth grain, some a hundredfold, some
> sixty, some thirty. He who has ears let him hear.   Matthew 13:3b-9

I am constantly amazed by conference speakers, evangelists, leaders and
many others, that will lead a session and declare the fields are white for
harvest. If they are describing the obvious state of lostness, then they are
correct. If they are interpreting the climate for spiritual harvest, they may
be dead wrong. Some areas are indeed ready for harvest; many are not!
What troubles me is that so many writers, theorists, and strategists don't
seem to know the difference. It is very easy for a guy, who is not involved in
the work of spiritual farming, to tell the laborers that they are surrounded
by folks just waiting to be harvested (saved). The truth is that this isn't true.
We have for too long listened to folks, who aren't fishing for men, tell us
how to fish, and even where the fish are biting. This might explain why so
many of our programs and methods have been so inept!

I remember many years ago, while I was serving as a youth pastor, our church brought in a departmental leader to lead us in evangelism training. For four nights he taught us with passion. On the fifth night we were scheduled to go out into the fields, "white" for harvest, to apply what we had been taught. When I asked with whom he was teaming up with, he told me he would stay behind and do the records. His not going told me volumes about his heart and belief. All week he had taught that people were just waiting to hear, if someone would but tell them, and the night we had that opportunity, he stayed behind! That is part of our dilemma. We have far to many people who have no idea what they are talking about telling us what the conditions are! If they are simply reporting the obvious, then fine, we live in a lost and dying world, but if they are telling us that the fields are ready to be harvested, they may be clueless.

As I have observed and worked the fields in which I have been called to serve, I have seen what I believe to be needful lessons concerning the parable of the sower. I am aware that the point for many is to just keep on sowing regardless of the soil—to which I say, amen! I am also aware that the seed is the gospel of the Kingdom of God. But rarely do we pay attention to the application of the soils for our given situation. For example, you may be serving in a really hard area. It is indisputable that the people all around you need Jesus. Any Christian can see that. But you may be working in the area of the beaten path or the rocky ground. You need to know that your results won't be like the guy working in the fertile fields of deep topsoil. You won't be asked to speak at evangelism programs; you won't have your picture taken with significant leaders, but you just might be called to such a hard place. You would never say it is ripe for harvest, while all the while you are mindful of the lostness of those around you.

In the place I serve I find hard to thorny ground. If I was content to reach folks from the South, I might interpret my soil differently, but that would be transfer growth, not transformational growth, and I am after the latter. I have also discovered that I can get people to pray prayers where they supposedly give their lives to Jesus almost daily, but then one has to realize they aren't being transformed. They want Jesus, but they aren't going to stop living with their girlfriend or smoking pot or anything else. They simply prayed a prayer; they are rocky ground. Some won't even give you the time of day. To them Christianity is a just another source of guilt and does nothing to enhance their lives. They are the path. Others want Jesus; they just want everything the world has to offer also. They can't say no to their indulgences. They want all the gusto this world can offer them. They eat and drink and live for the merry! They want to look "buff" and "beautiful," so whatever it takes to keep them looking good they are willing to do it. They have plastic surgeons and personal trainers, but they want to go to heaven when they can fit it into their schedule. These are the thorny ground people.

> Those who speak in terms of a great harvest just waiting to happen are many times delusional and nothing more than dreamers who don't understand the soils of their world.

The hardened path, the rocky ground and the thorny ground represent difficult soils with minimal, if any, harvest. They tragically perhaps represent the majority of soils found in the USA and Europe. Those who speak of our lostness and need for the gospel are accurate. Those who speak in terms of a great harvest just waiting to happen are many times delusional and nothing more than dreamers who don't understand the soils of their world. Some are just totally driven by their eschatology and therefore have no time to pay attention to facts.

None of those mentioned (soil types) people are waiting in line to follow Jesus. They aren't eagerly waiting for someone to tell them of their darkness and then how to find light. That they are lost is apparent; the idea that they are just waiting to be saved is erroneous. In my denomination much of what we have historically called evangelism has simply been the conversion of our own families. With the reduction of the average family size, guess what also drops—evangelism statistics and baptisms! We have never really been good at interpreting with what type of soil we are working. We have been fairly good at trying to do evangelism, but we have also gone with "one-size-fits-all" methods, which just don't work.

If you talk to a farmer or simply observe farming, you can learn some very important things about this parable. First, bad soil can over time become fertile, but it is costly and labor intensive. Second, even good soil needs moisture, and droughts come to fertile areas. Third, when it is time to harvest, harvest. Make hay while it is still daylight. Fourth, the farmer will harvest wherever there are plants ready to harvest. Some will bear minimum fruit, some maximum, but you still harvest where you are. Dry land farming may only yield a few bushels of wheat per acre during drought, while land near by that is irrigated will bear significantly more. Farmers always plant with the expectation of harvesting, but they are aware that some areas will yield more than others. We would do well to learn the same. I am aware that God can grow crops from rocks; He just doesn't do it very often!

> Don't stop working the fields; just don't let someone else's ignorance discourage you!

The point of all of this is for you to pay attention to your particular environment, and properly assess it through prayer, and determine what you are working with. Let your reality direct your need as you pray for God's provision and power. Don't let others tell you what you have before you, especially if they are clueless. Don't stop working the fields; just don't let someone else's ignorance discourage you!

A lot of people come from the South to the state in which I live. They come with great expectations of a bountiful harvest and building significant churches with great numerical growth. Why? Because this is what they are told exists or idealistically chose to believe! They rarely make it more than 4 years and then are "called" back to the south, to its security, its cultural Christianity and the "known." Beware of those making wild predictions of harvest.

I have only met a few young church planters who I believe grasp this concept in our area. One of the planters knows his soil is the hardened path, and therefore it will be hard and slow. I think he will make it and someday see what God has done through his faithfulness and steady working the fields. Most never pay any attention. They are going to start campus churches, cell churches or whatever churches, but when the money runs out, so do they. They never learn about the soils. Some will fail at church planting and get jobs as strategists for church planting, simply perpetuating the ignorance of our day.

God ultimately determines the harvest, but learn from the soils. If you are planted in a hard area, pray and work, pray and sow, pray and go and remember that you are not in competition with anyone but are called to be faithful in the field God has planted you. Again any soil can be made productive with prayer, cultivation and adequate irrigation. Need we mention the need for the *sun?*

I grieve when I see manmade strategies dictated by eschatology that cause us to de-emphasize fertile fields and true opportunities for great harvest, to focus on the hard, rocky and thorny grounds of our world. We should give them attention, but not at the expense of the fertile fields. Remember, fertile fields can be taken over by thorns or beaten down into paths if neglected. We must not miss the harvest of one area for the dream and hope of another. We must also seek out those who are truly strategists, based on their wisdom and experience in farming the harvest of God, not just the promotion of the methods of men. Jesus did say that the harvest is abundant but that there was a shortage of workers, in Matthew 9:37, therefore, we obviously need more workers! But I pray that the workers of the future may be wiser than we have perhaps tended to be. Dear friend, farm on!

What About My Marriage?

Now concerning the matters about which you wrote. It is well for a man not to touch a woman. But because of the temptation to immorality, each man should have his own wife and each woman her own husband. The husband should give to his wife her conjugal rights, and likewise the wife to her husband. For the wife does not rule over her own body, but the husband does; likewise the husband does not rule over his own body, but the wife does. Do not refuse one another except perhaps by agreement for a season, that you may devote yourselves to prayer; but then come together again, lest Satan tempt you through lack of self-control. I say this by way of concession, not of command.

1 Corinthians 7:1-6

To the unmarried and the widows I say that it is well for them to remain single as I do. But if they cannot exercise self control, they should marry. For it is better to marry than to be aflame with passion.

1 Corinthians 7:8-9

Wives, be subject to your husbands, as to the Lord. For the husband is the head of the wife as Christ is the head of the church, his body, and is himself its Savior. Even so husbands should love their wives as their own bodies. He who loves his wife loves himself. For this reason a man shall leave his father and mother and be joined to his wife, and the two shall become one flesh.

Ephesians 5:22-23, 28-29, 31

Marriage is a choice! It is a decision that two people make, hopefully within the scope of what they believe to be the will of God, and not on the basis of sexual indulgence. However, it is still a choice. There is this idea that floats around Christendom that a man is not complete without a wife and vice versa. This idea is wrong. If I look for another person to complete me, I am doomed to a life of frustration. If I look for a person to partner life with me and walk with me, I might be all right. Probably no area is more challenging than the area of marriage.

It has been very difficult for me over the years to see the church consistently feminizing men. Many of the hypersensitive, "emotionally-in-touch-religiously-correct" rebuke men for being men and say God wants them to be something God never intended for them to be. I have been to countless conferences led by weeping, bleeding-hearted guys that I wish would just get a grip on their emotions and be men. I have seen their wives just stare at them as they spoke, hanging on every word, as if this were the first time they heard them speak. Ugh! Men are told to get in touch with their emotions and to become more sensitive, gentle, compassionate, more like Jesus. I wonder just which Jesus they are referring to.

> When men abdicate their responsibility and women assume the headship position we are in sin, and this has been a problem since the beginning.

My personal theory about marriage begins in Eden after the fruit has been sampled. I think the curse still has ramifications to this day. My wife says that if God had created woman first there would have been no reason for man. She may be right, but the fact is God created man first. Part of the curse is that man will rule over woman and she is to be subjugated to him, in a distortion of God's original intent. Just suppose for one moment that women really are for the most part, more talented, better at multi-tasking, better parents, etc. and now God says for all time you will be under the rule of the man. Wow, what a difficult pill to swallow! That issue has been a rub ever since. I think that men don't want the responsibility, and women don't want to surrender control. You may think this is an over simplification, but I think it is a core issue. When men abdicate their responsibility and women assume the headship position we are in sin, and this has been a problem since the beginning. Add to this mix the feminization of the Christian male and you have a formula for trouble and discontent. I might add that it appears to be more peaceful (the ol' make-love-not-war in the marriage context!) to reverse the roles, but it will come at a huge cost, because it is a violation of the Word of God, and negates God's will in the marriage.

I have heard many Christian women speakers suggest that every Christian woman wants to submit to a Godly man, and for the most part I think this is just not the case. I can't think of an exception to what I am about to say. Every woman I have heard teach on submission knows nothing about it, because her husband leads only as she has permitted! If it weren't so tragic, it would be funny! I have never heard a submitted woman talk on submission. I have met and heard a lot of domineering women give their husbands permission to look like a man within reason. Their husbands act like little puppy dogs waiting on their owner to give them a little treat at the end of the day!

> Headship is not about control or bossing your wife around. It is about leadership, direction, and God's will.

I have also seen those men who "practice" headship over their docile wife. That shell of a person they call their spouse, that person whom they have broken by verbally and perhaps even physically abusing into a perceived state of submission. This is a crime and has nothing to do with what God has called men to be about! Headship is not about control or bossing your wife around. It is about leadership, direction, and God's will. It is to be patterned after Christ and His love for the church, which also presents a problem. If we truly look at the church, we see an ongoing problem of disobedience and lack of submission to Christ.

Insecure men make horrible husbands, and even worse leaders, because of their propensity to abuse those who have been entrusted to them. Headship does require gentleness and kindness. Headship demands sacrifice and love. Headship also points to the fact that the buck is to stop with the man as the Christ-like head of his home. Some churches teach a manhood and headship that has more in common with slavery. In God's design leadership and headship is about loving servitude, not control and dominance!

I have met some Christian women that fuel the fire of some men's dysfunction by believing they are to be forgiving, longsuffering and submissive regardless of what the husband does. This is ridiculous! God-called submission is never becoming a doormat for one's spouse to wipe the shoes of their immorality on. Many wives of another day tolerated the intolerable in the name of submission, when in reality it was thinking they had no way to live if they left or a way to support children of the marriage (I have heard ministers refer to this as good old days, with these biblical models of headship and submission!). How many bad marriages produced screwed up kids because momma thought she was obeying God? I can hear one of my peers saying, "Are you questioning God's will for marriage?" Not at all. I am suggesting that we stop calling people to do horrendous things in the name of biblical obedience.

Of course, this idea can work both ways. I remember a man whose wife turned out to be a lesbian. He was told that if he had only stayed with her and made her submit he could have saved her. This is so absurd, it isn't worth responding to! That said, I am going to leave the land of extremes to look at what is healthy and hopefully provide help.

Back to the premise for this chapter: God does have a plan for marriage with an eternal perspective. Men are to be the heads of their homes as Christ is the head of the Church and wives are to be submitted as the body is submitted to Christ. So how does this work? Men and women are as different as night and day. We really are from different planets. Our whole system is wired up differently from each other. This is what makes marriage so thrilling and challenging. It also makes it so very difficult and at times so very frustrating.

It begins with why we get married. The typical male marries the woman of his choosing or perhaps his dreams. Once he says "I do," he wants her to stay the same—same hair, same size, same sex appeal—stay the same! The wife marries her project. She loves the person she has wed and has demonstrated this through giving herself to him sexually. But she also sees a "D.I.Y." project, and she will spend the rest of your life helping you to become what she thinks you ought to be. By the way D.I.Y. is "do it yourself."

Another major complication in our time, and all times, is and has been the proliferation of premarital sex making a mess of marriage. It violates issues of trust, intimacy, and biblical obedience. There is no innocent premarital sex, even with the one I marry. It will carry consequences that will have to be addressed at some point down the road. It is tragic that we just assume couples will have sex before they are married.

> Women tend to be ahead of most men when it comes to grasping the meaning of "relationship," unless they are damaged by abuse.

We just accept that many young adults will have multiple sexual partners before they marry (this is true of Christians as well as non-Christians). If one looks at the beginnings of marriage, it was consummated at the point of intercourse. What does this say about moral carelessness and moral character? It says that the church, like our culture, is guilty of gross adultery. We have preached to the point of nausea against divorce, but we have rarely equated the same consequence to the immorally flagrant within our churches. What must God think when we condemn divorce but slap the hand of the "unmarried" sexually active?

Because men and women oftentimes enter into the relationship with very different experiences (including sexual), they bring radically different expectations to the marriage. The man is looking at spending time with his beautiful (always in the eye of the beholder!) wife, with whom he can have sex all the time. The wife is looking for emotional security and trust. She is looking for a person to share her heart with. Women tend to be ahead of most men when it comes to grasping the meaning of "relationship," unless they are damaged by abuse. The husband would just be happy if she watched an occasional football game with him and then left him alone. The wife is often looking for a non-sexual intimacy with kindness and tenderness. Most husbands are looking for "slam, bam, thank you, ma'am!" Many guys aren't looking for a friend; they already have those (though this is not always the case). They are looking for a sexual partner and a potential mother for their kids. This really is a gross over-simplification, but I hope you get the point. The unspoken expectations are the deadly ones. A spouse doesn't even know he/she is flunking because their mate just assumes she/he should know this stuff! Tacit expectations are deadly and should be avoided or confessed as often as they are discovered.

If marriage is so difficult, why bother? To be honest, some shouldn't, because they are basically selfish or just simply content in their singleness.

> Marriage is work, but work is good for us, and this particular job can be extremely gratifying.

The single person who is morally pure really has some ministry advantages. He or she can go places and do some things a married person can't. They can be more available and flexible, if they are not consumed with selfishness. They don't have to be concerned with their spouse's wishes or fears of kids; they can just go and do. This is exactly what Paul was talking about in 1 Corinthians 7, where he wished they could be as he was. There is a freedom in singleness that is surrendered when a person chooses to get married.

So, if singleness is preferable why marry? Again, some shouldn't, but marriage has great privilege and benefit that singleness cannot afford. Marriage allows better balance and a clearer focus on life. It allows one an intimacy that can only be discovered in a Christ-centered marriage. It allows one a partner to go through life and the potential of children, who truly are a gift from God, (at least when grown up!). An unmarried person just can't know this. Marriage is a great tool for helping us be concerned with the welfare of another, not just ourselves. It causes us to change; to change and hopefully become more sensitive to the needs of others. Marriage causes us to look at ourselves; why we do what we do, why we act as we do, why we think as we do and it forces us to adjust inappropriate stuff that is nothing more than baggage. Marriage ensures conflict that can work for our good, if we work at it and allow it. It assures us that we can't live just for ourselves anymore, nor should we. Marriage is work, but work is good for us, and this particular job can be extremely gratifying. But this satisfying relationship must be lived out in the context of God's purpose, and our roles must be fleshed out regardless of how difficult or dated they may seem.

If marriage is your reality, ask yourself, "Does your spouse share your heart for God?" Do you share your spouse's passion for the things of God? Are you partners in godliness and holiness? Remember, marriage was your choice. Hopefully, you biblically and prayerfully determined it to be God's will. This conclusion does not rule out problems and difficulties. It doesn't even alleviate divorce. It does however give us the hope of a Jesus-centered relationship, and if He is the center, it will be one that honors His Father.

If you believe you have a Christ-centered relationship, then who gives leadership? Where does the buck stop? This doesn't mean that the man is out there at the helm of the ship bearing it alone. It does mean, after listening to his bride and most of all God, he makes the decision. It does mean he is responsible for the direction of the marriage and family. The wife will give account for her willingness to allow her husband to truly lead. Will she encourage him to lead when he is reluctant or timid? Will she pray for him to become the man God desires him to be, and will she be content with that? Will she let this happen?

I remember a lady in a church I served saying, "my husband may be the head, but I am the neck that turns the head!" This is godless at its core. What is so tragic is that this lady sees herself as very submissive, when in reality she is the head, and her husband is just a shell of what God intended.

In marriage the question remains, will the man lead, and will the woman follow? Will he stand up and be a man in the image of Christ? Will she trust God to do what she can't and subsequently stop playing the Holy Spirit? Will the man become a man created in the image of Christ? Will the wife become as the Body of Christ? If she says, "Yes," and if he says, "Yes," a wonderful journey will begin. He has nothing to gloat about; God ordered this role; he didn't earn it. She is privileged to practice humility and look like her savior. She has nothing to resent; just be honored that God has allowed her to yield her rights as Christ yielded His.

The truth is a good marriage begins before two people say, "I do," and well before they engage in the holy act of sexual intimacy. Before God, were they both walking with God as best they understood the Scriptures? Was their relationship based on purity and moral integrity? Was Christ honored in the manner in which they entered marriage? Were they both pleasing Christ in their singleness?

Do you see Christ as your completer, or is that the role you have given your spouse? Remember, only Christ can complete, and He doesn't need help! Were you content to be unmarried, if that was what God wanted, or did you presume you were destined to marry the piano player or preacher? Both of the latter are very dangerous reasons to marry, but in fact they are all too frequently used! Were you the right person—were you focusing on God making you into the likeness of Jesus, or were you focused big time on your future spouse? One of my spiritual influences is a grand old man of God named John Crawford. John is a Navigator, who spent more time with Dawson Trotman than any other Navigator staff. John says, "If you want to marry the right person, be the right person!" Well, were you the right person?

> We had better be men who are willing to obey God above all and willing to lead our families to do the same.

Once you have determined the answer to the last question, marriage takes on a whole different perspective. I have watched couples, that came together just like any worldly couple, struggle with matters of obedience that shouldn't even have been an issue. I have seen men cry when they describe the unwillingness of their wives to go where they believe God is leading. Some won't leave a mother, a house, a town, or a state to the grief of their spouse. I have seen the remorse on the face of a wife who believed God had so much more for their marriage, only to see that promise quenched at the faithlessness of a disobedient husband. Choose wisely if you are single and thinking about marriage.

If you are married, are you able to do the things God is calling you to?

Are you afraid of the conflict obedience might cause? Men, you better obey the voice of God over any other voice. Why do we succumb to the voice of fear, faithlessness, cowardice, or the fear of what our spouse will do? Is God not greater than your spouse? Have you been a trustworthy leader? Have you earned your wife's respect and honor regardless of how she feels? For the most part, you must be sensitive to your wife and see her as your primary counsel, but ultimately, the bottom line is, will you obey God?

Some may say that God will never lead you to cross your spouse, but this is simply not true. Sometimes God will indeed speak through your spouse, and you, in wisdom, must hear her words and respond. Other times it will be like volumes of counsel have been given, but it is just personal wants and expressions. We had better be men who are willing to obey God above all and willing to lead our families to do the same.

I grieve over the huge number of Christian men who almost always surrender to the voice of their spouse regarding church, giving, membership, involvement, service, and ministry. This is a very dangerous yet prevalent pattern in the American church. Too many men of our generation have truly become men without chests and very little courage!

I haven't said anything about being sensitive and gentle and kind and compassionate. All of these things we should strive to be, but there are tons of books written about this stuff, all very important! I have heard women tell men what a women wants in a Christian husband (including my wife), which is also very important. But the voice I challenge you hear is the voice of God that calls you to be a man in the image of Christ! He calls us to be godly men not "girly boys," men of strength who care deeply and love passionately.

What About My Family?

Whoever does Gods will is my brother and sister and mother.

Mark 3:35 (NIV)

Do not think that I have come to bring peace on earth! I have not come to bring peace but a sword. For I have come to set a man against his father, and a daughter against her mother, and a daughter in law against her mother in law; and a man's foes will be those of his own household. He who loves father or mother more than me is not worthy of me and he who loves son or daughter more than me is not worthy of me; and he who does not take his cross and follow me is not worthy of me. He who finds his life will lose it, and he who loses his life for my sake will find it.

Matthew 10:34-39

So now I give him to the Lord. For his whole life he will be given over to the Lord.

1 Samuel 1:28 (NIV)

If any one comes to me and does not hate his own father and mother and wife and children and brothers and sisters, yes even his own life, he cannot be my disciple.

Luke 14:26

To another he said, "follow me." But he said, "Lord let me first go and bury my father." But he said to him, "Leave the dead to bury their own dead; but as for you, go and proclaim the kingdom of God." Another said, "I will follow you Lord; but let me first say farewell to those at my home." Jesus said to him, No one who puts his hand to the plow and looks back is fit for the kingdom of God.

Luke 9:59-62

What about my family? You can't be serious in asking me to make decisions that may be hard on my family? Do you think Jim Elliot's decision to visit a tribe known for their brutality and isolation was hard on his family? After all, it cost him and his co-laborers their lives. What about Hudson Taylor? How did it affect his family? He lost wives and children in a country that many would say was not his home. What about my family? After all, God gave me these children and this wife, and I must take care of them and my folks that need me to look after them. Do you read? What does the Scripture say? The Scripture is clear; we have just become dull of hearing. We refuse to believe that God could lead us to make hard decisions that could put our families in a financial or social or cultural hardship.

The disciples left everything, including their families, to follow Jesus. But we are convinced we are different, that what others have done is an aberration of the will of God for me. If you pick up your cross and follow, you select a different course for your life and that of your family. There are no exceptions. Regardless of the idolatry we in the church promote as the biblical mandate for the family. God's Word has much to say about our lives and those of our families. Just read the Book.

The biblical basis of marriage and family needs to start with your decision to pick up your cross and follow Jesus. It is rooted in our renouncing all and following Him. We, however, have reinterpreted the text, softened its demands and re-qualified its expectation for us. But for those who haven't, who really want to honor God in their families, there is much to be said. Before you start your family, consider the cost in terms of service, time, energy and monies. What does God want of you? Based on your willing obedience to follow, what is your life saying God wants? If one chooses to have a family, amen! Just be clear as to what God wants. "We are going to help raise up a Christian generation!" Please, this line of thinking is based on poor interpretation of the Old Testament and

> We refuse to believe that God could lead us to make hard decisions that could put our families in a financial or social or cultural hardship.

irresponsible faith. "We are going to have a ton of kids because we are commanded in Psalms 127:4-5 to have a quiver full of them!" Is this really a life application command? I think not! To me this is just bad theology and worse application. If you want a large family, have one, but make sure you have sought the true counsel of God's Word and wise mentors. I have seen ministries horribly reduced because of bad belief with sincere intent. I have seen the decision to have small or no families based on equally bad theology and many times just plain and simple selfishness. Regardless of one's choice regarding family, will it become a reason for me not to go or stay, obey or disobey? Will it cause me to "say farewell"? I have known those who say they will have kids so their kids will go in their place. Right! God doesn't want your firstborn. He wants your heart and obedience, and he wants your undivided attention.

The decision whether or not to have a family may have already been made. But will you obey God's will or fabricate one to fit your circumstance? Regardless of one's family size, the question is are you willing to pay the price necessary to do what God has laid on your heart to do? If you are unwilling to pay the price, you need not apply for service. I mean, if you have to be home by 4:00 p.m. and never work on weekends, you are already disqualified. There is a growing idea that ministry must take place around my child's schedule, or around my wife's work, or my own need to be mister mom. Please stop before you make a mockery of your calling.

The challenge for you is to maintain a proper tension. When a guitar string has the proper tension it is in tune. Are you in tune? If you are going to give too much time to the family, you are like a string strung loosely—it produces no note because there is not enough tension—and you will be spiritually flat. If you choose to go, go, go, you may be tuned, but be very sharp, and if too much tension is applied, the string will break. You'll burn out, burn up or blow up, but you will have a breakdown! Tragically, when the latter occurs, it has dire consequences on everything you love. The former doesn't break down, but it does bog down for lack of availability and obedience. You may have gone to all of little Johnny's ball practices, scrimmages, and games, but God has long since stopped trying to use you. To follow Christ doesn't ever mean one has to neglect his family, but it does mean there will be deliberate sacrifices made that have a definite price tag.

Long before you have kids, or perhaps where you are now, you must ask, "God will I leave all and follow you?" Will you choose the narrow way, even for your precious wife and children? Do you believe that the only way to find one's life is to lose it? Do you *really* believe this? Will you obey the clear teaching of Scripture or claim some spurious Bible promise that has nothing to do with anything except what you want? Are you and your wife on the same page? How do you know? If you asked her to move to Zambia as a career missionary, would she go or send you a post card on your birthday? If you asked her to leave her nice little home in the suburbs to live in a remote rural setting in the dusty West, would she go without strings or conditions? These are the subjects that need to be hammered out well before the discussion of marriage or family. These are the things that help clarify God's will for a relationship.

> To follow Christ doesn't ever mean one has to neglect his family, but it does mean there will be deliberate sacrifices made that have a definite price tag.

To my wife's credit I can say that she has never stopped me from doing what I believed was God's will for our family—better, what *we* believed was God's will for our family. She has consistently challenged me to make sure that it was God's voice I was listening to. After all, she would remind me, "You are the one who will have to stand before God and be held responsible." This isn't to say that she has been a quiet little church mouse never saying a word. She offers her needed input, her important view on the circumstance, her fear and faith, but she leaves the final call to me. I have never done or not done something because I didn't feel Dee was supportive. I have seen the wisdom in her counsel many times and as a result, I have made a decision that reflected my heeding her voice. However, she expects me to hear God above her voice and all other voices.

I have been privileged to pastor growing churches (never a mega-church) and the truth is it always comes at a personal sacrifice. Churches don't grow without sacrifice and if we aren't willing to pay it, we might reflect on just what we are called to do. Again, this is the difference between leadership and management, but that has already been discussed. Regardless, your sacrifice is required. Sacrifice is required that will affect your family, time and money. As my boys grew up, I missed a few baseball games, but not most. I attended a lot of their practices, and unless I was out of town, I never missed a big game. I would not miss my kid's game for a church committee meeting. I didn't have time to coach their teams, or go to every team meeting, nor did my wife. Our world did not revolve around their sports. I have hundreds of hours of my kids' games on video, and I am grateful for the time they were at home and in sports. But I am grateful that before they had my heart Jesus did, and his call came first. My kids don't suffer from dad not loving them or not being with them. The church didn't take their dad away, but sometimes I couldn't be there. It was hard to be at a game if I was in South America on a mission trip.

> By allowing Jesus to win, your family will win, even though you won't look like the family down the street.

I have also made it a rule that nothing but the death of an immediate family member or one of the church's key leaders, like an elder, would cause me to shorten or return early from a vacation with my family. If anyone else died or got sick, I'd just check on them and delegate the ministry to others. But I have no guilt about not allowing my world to revolve around my sons' sports calendar. If you have to be at every event or every game you probably have too much time.

The point that I am making is that to follow Christ will be costly, and you must decide if you will pay it or not. I have been told that what I am suggesting is just too hard. If counting the cost regarding my decisions about marriage and family are considered hard, then we are in trouble. Be sure that I am not talking about sacrificing for the sake of any method.

But I am saying that being faithful to the biblical mandate will come at a price. There are no exceptions, but there are plenty of guys in the ranks of ministry who have already conceded defeat because they aren't going to give what is required. I admonish you not to be one of those. Again, you don't have to neglect your family, but your family must know that your obedience to the great command of God and His great commission will always win. By allowing Jesus to win, your family will win, even though you won't look like the family down the street. You can't; you mustn't! Remember, our objective isn't to be like everyone else, but rather be conformed to Jesus our Lord. The price tag has never changed, it will cost you all that you hold dear and love, but the exchange rate is wonderful!

Finally, let it be said that your family is a precious gift, but your love for them must pale in comparison to your love for Christ. You have one good shot to give your family, so why not give them a living sacrifice rather than Mr. Cleaver? Why not give them more than the world can offer? It will be hard, but it will be in tune. There will be plenty of tension, but the dividends are worth it! You can't determine your child's outcome; that will be their choice, but you can give them the right tools to make the right decisions. I guess a person can claim a Proverb as a promise, but the outcome of your child has more to do with their choice than you being at every ball practice. It has more to do with you giving them your heart for God than always being there. Young boys and girls will grow up and admire a father who loved God first above mom and them. Again, don't confuse neglect with this, because they aren't the same. Count the cost. Are you willing to pay it? Then God bless you. If not, may God help you!

Doctrine Really Matters

Do your best to present yourself to God as one approved, a workman who has no need to be ashamed, rightly handling the word of truth.

2 Timothy 2:15

All scripture is inspired by God and profitable for teaching, for reproof, for correction, and for training in righteousness, that the man of God may be complete, equipped for every good work.　2 Timothy 3:16-17

We live in a time like those days before us, where it really does matter what you believe. My denomination, Southern Baptists, tolerate a tension between a purported old SBC belief in Calvinism and a mainstream classical Baptist view, i.e., a view that man has a free will, God is Sovereign and yet He allowed Christ to die for all that all might be saved. But unlike the Calvinist, we believe that God allows man to choose. Man can receive the free gift of God, eternal life through faith in Christ, or man can reject it and hope there is no hell! God knows the outcome but that is a far cry from determining the outcome. The truth is these two views aren't compatible, and they will eventually lead to a breakdown in the ranks. No one wants that, but I predict it will be inevitable because the systems are not compatible. It will be as inevitable as was the conservative-liberal (moderate) battles of the 1970s and '80s.

To my shame, I was in my early days totally turned off to anything that smelled of doctrine, not realizing that I was fleshing out my doctrine on a daily basis. It was doctrine that, to no small degree, brought an end to the generic Jesus Movement. Though it was a great experience it became increasingly difficult to attempt to reconcile so many varied and sometimes heretical beliefs. Though I started off as a Charismaniac, I later discovered I had huge issues with much of what are now common Charismatic teachings. In my personal journey I investigated doctrines like losing one's salvation, baptism of the Holy Spirit with the evidence of speaking in tongues, the issues of healings, signs and wonders. I discovered after about two years I had problems with most of these issues from a doctrinal point. These aren't minor issues and they can cause division and confusion. I also was confronted with the five points of Calvinism, which also inspired much study. I personally believe that the Charismatics and the Calvinists represent the extremes of Christian Protestantism. I am acutely aware of the significance of John Calvin to the Reformation, but I also believe he would be hugely broken over what his belief system has evolved into.

For much of what we disagree about, salvation is not at stake but sometimes it is. Does it matter who baptizes you? Is salvation dependent on whether or not I think the Lord's Cup turns in to His "real" blood or is simply symbolic? Is baptism a part of the salvation act? Does God predestine people for His wrath and His salvation? Can a person really be lost and saved multiple times? These are the doctrinal issues that divide us, and honestly should, as far as regular worship and fellowship are concerned. They should not divide us as brothers. I have over the years enjoyed the fellowship of godly brothers who were from the Presbyterians, the Methodists, the Lutherans, the Assemblies of God, the Evangelical Free and many independents. We focused on our common bond, Jesus, but we would not have agreed with nor enjoyed some of the particulars of each other's belief system. I choose to look at the differences as a demonstration of God's uniqueness and largeness of His family. We are united in the central things, divided at the fringe. However, this is not always the case.

Does it matter if Adam and Eve had wings? Does it matter if a TV evangelist doesn't believe in the Trinity? Does it matter if one of the super-

> I personally believe that the Charismatics and the Calvinists represent the extremes of Christian Protestantism.

church pastors never ever teaches on obedience, discipline, cost and the cross? The answer is, emphatically, yes it does matter! The problem with too many is that we are too fast to embrace, to fast to call one a brother, to quick to affirm without first checking out their message. We in my own denomination are too quick to affirm some, while just as quick to burn others. I can remember a few years back when Rick Warren was castigated by his own; now he is the poster child. He hasn't changed, but the monies he has given changed everything to his critics. Yet, there needs to be caution (not with Rick!).

I have observed many young pastors and church planters come along in my denomination, who had never read the *Baptist Faith and Message.* Consequently, they have no idea what we believe, and what we believe defines us! I have watched as church planters have aligned with us who came from Presbyterian backgrounds, Charismatic, and others. Unless they have had a major doctrinal change, they aren't Baptist, yet they are operating under the Baptist umbrella. I am sure this is not unique to Baptists, but it does cause undue hardship later. When doctrine is minimized it creates confusion and dishonors God. However, it must be understood, that no one group has the market on doctrinal purity or rightness. I affirm, for the most part, the *Baptist Faith and Message* (confessing my bias as a Southern Baptist) when it presents biblical principle. Worship styles, type of music, liturgy, are all issues that express preference and are not as important as key doctrinal issues.

> When looking at doctrinal issues and positions, we must know the difference between principle and method.

When looking at doctrinal issues and positions, we must know the difference between principle and method. For example, in many circles expositional preaching is presented as a biblical principle. It is not. Expositional preaching is a very good method, but it is simply a method. Sunday School, evangelism programs, times of services, types of songs, use of hymnals are all issues regarding method and preference, not principle and therefore, not doctrine. They may present doctrine, embrace doctrine, and reveal doctrine, but the package is about method, not principle.

I think it is critical to look at the relationship between a biblical principle or doctrine and distinguish it from pet methods. For example, in SBC churches, the *Baptist Faith and Message* espouses congregational rule as the biblical model for church leadership and polity. This is our historical preference. The problem is that it is not a principle at all, but rather a method. The *Baptist Faith and Message* is full of doctrinal positions and biblical principles, but on occasion it confuses our methods with our doctrine. Another example is the Cooperative Program. This is an outstanding way of doing missions, but it is not a principle. Missions is the principle, the Cooperative Program is a method to carry out the biblical principle. We sometimes, however, treat the program with more reverence than the doctrinal mandate for missions. The infallibility of the Scriptures is a biblical principle and a doctrinal position. It was at the core of what we, as Southern Baptist fought over in the '70s and '80s, and, fortunately, those who knew the difference between true principle and method, and the difference between doctrine and man centered ideas, won the war!

In a day of theological hodgepodge and even a huge dose of theological post-modernism, we must be all the more clear about our doctrinal beliefs. We must be clear about the difference between a biblical principle and methodology. It is true that it is sometimes our methods, like the Cooperative Program of Southern Baptists, that truly makes us unique. But it is our doctrine that reveals who we are by exposing what shapes our belief. In the '70s and '80s some tried to make the issue our methodology to hide the underlying biblical issues, but our issue wasn't over methods. It is true that, for the most part, too many of us we are more prone to fight over a sacred cow method, than a position of doctrinal truth!

For me, it does matter if a person is a Calvinist. The very tenets of their belief system put them at odds with many of the tenets of being Baptist. The same is true with being a closet Charismatic within the context of a Baptist church. Some Calvinists will point to C.H. Spurgeon as an example of Baptist Calvinism. He was also purported to be bipolar. Is that something we should associate with being a good Baptist? The doctrine of perseverance has a real conflict of interest with eternal security, unless I force it to fit and do a massive reinvention of its proposals (as some try to do)! This is equally true of the Charismatic teaching on the Holy Spirit; it just doesn't fit in a Baptist suit! If one wants to be Calvinist, great! It just needs to be in that community of belief. If one wants to be Charismatic, great! It, too, needs to be with those who hold those doctrines to be true. But I am puzzled that some get really upset over Baptist churches that incorporate elder leadership but say nothing over Calvinism. This is insane to me, but it is consistently human!

Finally, the point I make is, be true to the one you are with! Don't try to make something fit just because you want to or have traditionally done something. There is a great need for biblical understanding and even diversity, but we can't integrate all doctrinal positions under one tree, and it is wrong to think we can. The family of God is a diverse and colorful family, so it calls us to doctrinal integrity. Be true to what you believe in the context of biblical parameters.

> There is a great need for Biblical understanding and even diversity, but we can't integrate all doctrinal positions under one tree, and it is wrong to think we can.

Never go beyond what the Scripture allows; submit to its authority; recognize that all will not agree, and again, be true to what you believe.

Children try to force others to join their side or pout and go home. In a day of greater than ever lostness, we must be unified at the point of orthodoxy but different at the point of alignment. We can work together, but that doesn't mean we have to share the same bed. Celebrate our differences where they are biblically defendable positions, but recognize it is OK to simply be cousins. If you are a Charismatic, be one! If you are Calvinist, be one! If you are a Baptist, be one! Be true to the Word and yourself and stop trying to squeeze folks into your mold! Align with what is consistent to the principles and doctrines you hold, don't try to be what you aren't or argue that everyone else is wrong except you! Doctrine matters. What does your doctrine say about you?

Speaking of doctrine, this might be an appropriate place to mention a non-doctrine issue for me—my use of the Revised Standard Version. I am aware that some have major issues with the RSV. I began memorizing the RSV while in seminary in 1977. Prior to seminary I had memorized the KJV, so I welcomed the RSV as a translation that brought added clarity to my understanding. Though I am aware of its weaknesses, I am a firm believer that it is still the infallible Word of God. I am also aware that some even have problems with the New International Version. I think it safe to say that there are those among us conservatives that just have to have something to have a problem with!

The Times They are Changing!

Preach the Word; be prepared in season and out of season; correct,
rebuke, and encourage—with great patience and careful instruction.

2 Timothy 4:2 (NIV)

As for you, always be steady, endure suffering, do the work of an
evangelist, fulfil your ministry.

2 Timothy 4:5

Practice these duties, devote yourself to them, so that all may see
your progress. Take heed to yourself and to your teaching; hold to that,
for by so doing you will save both yourself and your hearers.

1 Timothy 4:15-16

"The times they are a-changin'." Bob Dylan and the Byrds back in the 1960s
sang about this fact of changing times in the world—and to this changing
world I hope you have been called. We live in day of rapid, constant change
and ongoing technological advancement. We live in a state of flux. Much
of the change is exciting and helpful; some is simply scary! How will we be
the church in the midst of a world of change without compromising our
souls? This calls us to be harder on ourselves and the charge we have been
given. How do we penetrate the lostness of a society that rapidly has fewer
and fewer points of reference for us to address? There is obviously no single
answer, but we do hold the answer.

I remember what Charlie Riggs, who worked many years with the
Billy Graham team, once said in an interview, "Your life is your ministry."
To which I would add, your life is also your message. In a day that by in

large rejects the idea of absolute truth, we are called to live, preach and teach it. There has never been a day where this is more apparent or needful. Until we start producing better men and women of God, all of the methodologies in the world along with all of our money won't matter. Seminaries are helpful tools, but they cannot do what only God can do—make us into the persons we need to be to make a difference in this age. There can be no wavering or compromise in our resolve. We must be people who know and live the absolute truth of God's Word.

Speaking of methods, we have got to learn the difference between methods and principles. It is obvious in my own denomination that we sometimes confuse the two. We tend to enshrine our methods, from traditional orders of worship to Sunday School and completely miss the principle of making disciples. We must know that doing evangelism is a principle, but how we do evangelism reveals the method we choose, and not all methods work well in all areas. But if we are to make a difference, and I believe we are and will, we must rethink our strategies to better communicate our principles, rather than constantly showcasing our methods and programs. This is a rub for some, since their whole existence is to promote man-made methods, and this sometimes comes at the cost of the principle it purports to promote.

The times are changing and changing quickly. The church is also changing. Some of this is good and needful. Some of our change is regrettable. Some groups, to fit into our western culture have forsaken their biblical moorings. We must not do this. Some have compromised principle to relate—something we must be careful to avoid doing. I played in a classic rock 'n' roll band for a number of years. Why? To get into places that would not normally invite Christians to speak. We would use the music as a key to get people's attention and then share our testimonies of Christ's transforming power. We saw hundreds come to Christ in jails, prisons, fairs, biker rallies, church-sponsored lake parties and many church-sponsored block parties. We would use the music to share the gospel with folks who wouldn't come into a church building. Most would come for the music and then also listen intently to the gospel and testimonies. Over the years we saw hundreds come to the saving knowledge of Christ. We took the gospel literally to very dark places, but we were careful not to compromise our biblical principles and mandate to evangelize.

The point of the music was to share the gospel with everyone who came to hear the music. We didn't play in church services but rather on the streets and in prisons, where most church folks don't go. The point of this story is that because we played rock and roll, a couple of church planters heard of us. They wanted us to play at a "church sponsored beer party." They didn't want us sharing our testimonies, preaching, or anything blatantly Christian; they just wanted rock and roll music. We declined in a heartbeat. I told the guys they had the wrong band for the job. They were shocked at our rejection of their offer. We were not interested in playing a rock and roll gig unless we could use it to share the gospel. The music was simply a tool to communicate the principle. They, in the name of being able to relate, were willing to negotiate and negate what we considered a non-negotiable. To relate we just have to be truthful and faithful, which is more important than fitting in with the crowd.

> To date, we have either stood rigid, mandating that the world adhere to our methods, or we have assimilated to become the very people we have been called to reach.

In this day of change we must not negate our principles, and our convictions must be biblically based. It is a great time for us to re-evaluate some of our methods, but I fear we won't. We must not give up what is most important. I was at a conference where the speaker said Bono, the lead singer for U2, is the prophet of our day. He might be a prophet for the obvious, but his must not be the voice we give our attention to. Bono might help us understand some things about our day, but he is not a messenger we should listen to. Paul put it well, in the ninth chapter of first Corinthians, where he said he had become all things to all men that by all means he might save some. That must become our motto. To date, we have either stood rigid, mandating that the world adhere to our methods, or we have assimilated to become the very people we have been called to reach. What are we willing to do to reach this generation? The times are changing; what are we prepared to do?

I hope that this writing will be received for what it is—one man's journey as a pastor and as a disciple maker. The experiences are mine but not unique to me. The absolute truth of Scripture is eternal, never changing, non-negotiable and true for all of us!

I conclude with some significant words of counsel from the Word of God which are fitting for times such as ours:

> With what shall I come before the Lord and bow myself before God on high? Shall I come before him with burnt offerings, with calves a year old? Will the Lord be pleased with thousands of rams, with ten thousands of rivers of oil? Shall I give my first born for my transgression, the fruit of my body for the sin of my soul? He has shown you. O man, what is good; and what does the Lord require of you but to do justice and to love kindness, and to walk humbly with your God?
>
> Micah 6:6-8

> The end of the matter; all has been heard. Fear God, and keep his commandments; for this is the whole duty of man.
>
> Ecclesiastes 12:13

> For though I am free from all men, I have made myself a slave to all, that I might win the more. To the Jews; I became as a Jew, in order to win Jews; to those under the law I became as one under the law—though not being myself under the law—that I might win those under the law. To those outside the law I became as one outside the law-not being without the law toward God but under the law of Christ-that I might win those outside the law. To the weak I became weak, that I might win the weak. I have become all things to all men, that I might by all means save some.
>
> 1 Corinthians 9:19-22

Bibliography

Barna, George. *Today's Pastors: A Revealing Look at What Pastors are Saying About Themselves, Their Peers and the Pressures They Face.* Ventura: Regal Books, 1993

Barna, George. *Growing True Disciples: New Strategies for Producing Genuine Followers of Christ.* Colorado Springs: Waterbrook Press, 2001

Cloud, Henry and John Townsend. *Safe People.* Grand Rapids: Zondervan, 1995

Coleman, Robert E. *The Master Plan of Discipleship.* Old Tappan: Fleming H. Revell Company, 1987

Coleman, Robert E. *The Master Plan of Evangelism.* Old Tappan: Fleming H. Revell Company, 1976

Hendricks, Howard and William Hendricks. *As Iron Sharpens Iron: Building Character in a Mentoring Relationship.* Chicago: Moody Press, 1995

Kotter, John P. *Leading Change: An Action Plan From the Worlds Foremost Expert on Business Leadership.* Boston: Harvard Business School Press, 1996

Kouzes, James M. and Barry Z. Posner. *The Leadership Challenge.* San Francisco: Jossey-Bass, 1997

McIntosh, Gary and Samuel D. Rims Sr. *Overcoming the Dark Side of Leadership.* Grand Rapids: Baker Books, 1997

Maxwell, John. *Falling Forward: Turning Mistakes Into Stepping Stones for Success.* Nashville: Nelson, 2000

McManus, Erwin Raphael. *An Unstoppable Force: Daring to Become the Church God had in Mind.* Loveland: Group Publishing, 2001

McNeal, Reggie. *The Present Future: Six Tough Questions for the Church.* San Francisco: Jossey-Bass, 2003

McNeal, Reggie. *A Work of Heart: Understanding How God Shapes Spiritual Leaders.* San Francisco: Jossey-Bass, 2000

McSwain, Larry L. and William C Treadwell Jr. *Conflict Ministry in the Church.* Nashville: Broadman Press, 1981

Oswald, Roy and Otto Kroeger. *Personality Type and Religious Leadership.* Washington, DC: Alban Institute, 1996

Petersen, Jim. *Lifestyle Disicpleship.* Colorado Springs: NavPress, 1993

Peterson, Eugene H. *Working the Angles.* Grand Rapids: Eerdmans Publishing Co, 2000

Tillapaugh, Frank R. *Unleashing the Church: Getting People Out of the Fortress and into Ministry.* Ventura: Regal Books, 1982

Willard, Dallas. *The Divine Conspiracy: Rediscovering Our Hidden Life in God.* New York: HarperCollins Publishers, 1998